BUFFGRUNT

Memoirs of a Tree Vet

Tommy J Skiens

TOMMY J. SKIENS

ISBN: 0-615-61358-6
ISBN-13: 978-0-615-61358-1

Acknowledgement

For their generous support:

Victor Volkman, Earnest Dempsey, Marc Levy, Rich Raitano, D. Russel Micnhimer, Peggy Molner, Claudia Pereira, Terrac Skiens, Linnea Coleman, Mike Christenson, Drew Mendelson, Fred Waterman /veteran/friend

Tommy J Skiens

Dedication

This work is dedicated to my four grandchildren. I hope they come to know and appreciate all forms of art.

A war buffs

(Book bonus)

As a digital gift and paperback book bonus I would like to offer you the opportunity to follow an infantry Battalion in combat during the Vietnam War. The SITREPS contained at this link; http://www.buffgrunt.com.

Provide documents for every casualty producing event encountered by the Forth Battalion of the Third Infantry Regiment for a 46 month period beginning December 1967 and including parts of October 1971.

The daily staff journals linked to each battalion casualty producing event covered on the buffgrunt.com website have been collected, one at a time, in a dimly lit environment with a camera at the national archives by veterans of the Americal Division. Over eleven thousand pages of documents have been retrieved from the national archives that are directly related to the 4/3. The result is literally a digital piece of history accessible to anyone who cares to take the time to honor these men from one of the oldest infantry regiments in United States military history. The men of the Old Guard earned the nick name, buff straps during the Civil War. These men are and will remain the honor guard at the Arlington National cemetery and the tomb of the Unknown Soldier.

CONTENTS

Introduction

I am writing this memoir before I die because it will be extremely difficult to get a good internet connection afterwards.

Those of us born shortly after WW II have been dubbed the, "Baby Boomers". Our global generation was in diapers as the world regained its footing after destroying parts of Africa, Europe, Asia and the Pacific. We called the WW II survivors, "The Greatest Generation", and many of them would later call some of us hippies, commies and fags for exercising our first amendment rights to protest the wars in Vietnam and Iraq. It seemed like they were saying, "America, land of one voice. Love the voice or leave the land". Some of the people being called names were patriotic like me and had joined the military to become combat veterans in American uniforms. Some of the people who practiced name calling never sacrificed one second of their lives for America but they rushed to buy flags and hide behind deferments or the National Guard while cheering on the drum beaters who would profit from armed conflict.

For two years I served in the active military but the 362 days I lived in Vietnam has dominated my life . Civilians tell us to forget about the war; get a job and start a family, they say. They tell us this because they really don't really don't care. They don't want to know the truth about war or trauma. They don't want to know what a 19 year old American soldier is capable of doing to unarmed women and children. They seek the fantasy or the movie where everything has a happy ending. Well America, this story has a happy ending but you might have to strap on a pair of boots before you get there.

Lend me a hand

During the biggest part of my twenty year career with the USDA, Forest Service, I was on a timber marking crew. This might possibly have been the best job in the world given my severe PTSD, post traumatic stress disorder. I found the PTSD in Vietnam and it latched onto me like a lonely stray puppy. The PTSD insists on hanging around even after I discover how to surround it with Veteran Administration provided medications that I will take until I get to old to swallow. The medications are delivered to me in the mail by people who are famous for going postal. I find it ironic that the people best known for going postal put meds in my mailbox so I won't. It is as if they have a franchise on the act and if I copy them I would be in violation of some law and I could get in trouble.

The timber marking crew boss, four workers and myself, would pile into the green crew cab pick-up at 7:00 in the morning and drive to a unit of a timber sale on the National Forest. Upon arriving at the unit we would fill our vests with 20 to 30 lbs. of two pound paint cans, our lunch, water, maps and other equipment. This was a lot like what I did in Vietnam except no one was dying. I would pack a bunch of weight on my back and hump all day up and down hills. Instead of an M-16 I carried a tree marking paint gun. It was like having a picnic in the forest every day. I loved that job.

Approximately one year after graduating from the Veterans Administration's six week drug and alcohol treatment program in Roseburg Oregon I had an experience with the marking crew that dropped me to my knees. Fortunately the crew boss was a Vietnam veteran who had served on a ship in the Gulf of Tonkin. He was a man of faith and a friend. He is still on my winners list. If I ever win the lottery he will get a piece of the prize.

After finishing the loading up of my vest with paint and equipment on this particular day I had moved thirty feet away from the crew to smoke one last cigarette before we entered the woods. I was squatting like the gooks in Vietnam who invented hemorrhoids. My legs were spread just beyond shoulder width, my feet were flat on the ground and my knees were bent at a severe angle allowing my butt to be suspended inches above the earth.

As I looked through the smoke exiting my mouth I happened upon a male crew member preparing his vest. I saw that his right arm was a bloody stump just above the elbow. My heart rate exploded and I began breathing in labored short hurried gasps. My fists were clinched in a fight of flight response to the intrusion and the palms of my hands were moist from anxiety. I closed my eyes and shook my head to rid myself of the intrusive mental image. I opened my eyes again and looked at a female crew member. The left side of her face was burnt to the bone. I could see her skull, empty eye socket and teeth exposed through the melted flesh. I was having a major flash back in the broad day light. I was also having a minor anxiety attack.

I moved further away from the crew to protect them from my flash back. I wanted to get into the woods as soon as possible. I should be more careful about what I want. As soon as I moved into my strip of timber I started seeing gooks behind the trees. I stopped trying to mark timber and began moving from one cover to the next in staggered quick bursts. I was freaked out.

Along came the crew boss. He was tall, slow and steady. He had noticed that something was not right with me at our staging area. He came into my strip to check things out. I didn't have the words to tell him what was happening. Intrusive mental images were years away from my vocabulary and understanding. I thought flashbacks were about things we remembered and I didn't remember seeing a female with half her face burnt off. I understood the bloody stump because I had been there and seen that several times.

We talked about what had happened. I said that I knew where the severed limb had come from but it was not supposed to be here in Oregon. The part that bothered me most was the melted flesh on the female skull. I could not remember ever seeing such a site in Vietnam. I was a mess and the crew boss understood. I don't know how far he went to protect me over the years but he is still on my winners list. He gave me a hand when I needed it. The phrase, lend me a hand, has other meanings for me as well.

The flash back occurred about 20 years after I returned from Vietnam. Fifteen years after the flashback I was building the website for the fourth battalion of the Old Guard when I came across some radio communication between Charlie Company and the battalion tactical operation center. The radio conversation reported finding two bodies in a shallow grave, one Chinese male and one Vietnamese female with half her face burnt off. The report also said there were five hands in the grave. The five hands sparked a memory that would become complete over time. There was something I was trying to understand here. My mind slowly filled in the details and fiction provided the glue. All the names used in this account of the burial flashback are fictional.

1968

Harold stood with his legs spread slightly apart and his hands on his hips. "This is far out", he said as he looked down at the growing collection of body parts scattered on the ground.

"It is always good to have an extra hand when you have some heavy lifting to do," said Norman, the fire team joker.

Tom chuckled as he slowly shook his head from side to side. He was curiously dismayed and seeking reason for yet another combat related mystery. The exposed grave had revealed two bodies and five hands. Where did the extra hand come from?

"Yo breeze, give me a hand pulling this gook out of the hole," Richard requested.

Norman grabbed the severed hand and pitched it toward Richard while the other grunts hooted and laughed.

"You're one sick mother-fucker," Richard offered as he picked the hand up and chucked it back toward the pile.

Jeff intercepted the hands flight with his entrenching tool and batted it into what would have been left field if this were a baseball game and the hand was a ball. The crowd hooted and cheered its approval. Someone suggested the hit was a double while others thought it better; home run.

"You sick fuckers," said Richard as he extracted the last body out of the shallow grave.

About one hour earlier Charlie Company had passed through the shallow grave area in a forced march effort to reposition. The company commander had ordered a lieutenant to find out what the fresh dirt mounds contained. The Lieutenant had passed the order to a Specialist fourth class fire team leader. I hooked up with the fire team to see what was in the grave and also because I had a PRC- 25 radio which I am convinced is the most important weapon you can have in a war.

Most people who go to war are assigned a weapon of some sort. It might be no more than their prick which they would follow wherever it pointed. Others pack a .45 cal. Pistol or M-16 rifle. One man per fire team had an M-79 grenade launcher and one man per squad had an M-60 machine gun. A company in the field had a weapons platoon that packed an 81mm mortar. The radio provided communication for everyone. It could be used to bring damn-damn on the local population in the form of big mortars, artillery, gunships, fast movers and the Volkswagen-size ordinance from the battle ship Missouri. If Charlie threw a rock at us we could remove his entire province from the planet with the ordinance at the other end of my radio.

The fire team and I stood in a semi-circle taking inventory of the body parts removed from the grave.

Inventory item no. 1: Female, Vietnamese, very dead from multiple large shrapnel wounds. The left side of her face had been burnt severely so as to expose her skull and teeth.

Inventory item no. 2: Male, Chinese, very dead from shrapnel, over 6' tall, well dressed in a Chinese officer's uniform.

Inventory item no.3: The fifth hand in a two person grave.

The fifth hand in a two person grave and the melted female skull will be the catalyst for having intrusive mental images and flashbacks over twenty years later. Having a complete story helps calm those visions. I believe truth and exposure can neutralize many PTSD symptoms including nightmares and bouts of depression. Still, I wonder how I could ever have forgotten something this unique. You don't see things like this every day.

If I smile and have many puzzled thoughts running through my mind when someone asks me to give them a hand, allow me a minute to collect myself.

Sergeant Maddox

War stories are hard to tell, the emotion driven memories come in short foggy encounters. Their contents barley comprehensible to those innocent who have avoided the military and its greatest tool, war. It is not uncommon for dates, places and even the names of a dead best friend to succumb in the face of forgetfulness for the sake of the minds sanity. Pain in the heart of a man is a lonely unspoken truth. Etiquette demands a Warriors Pride in the recounting of the killing of another human being or the loss of a friend. We rarely talk about our own trauma induced pain. We are the secret smile at our best friend's funeral. We are the dead men who patrol a group's perimeter. And we are the children who dance in a cloud of human carnage.

My youth was filled with dreams of a war that would endow me with a crown of manhood and understanding. I received instead a war that brought to question my support and belief in the American system and demonstrated the irrational cruelty of a 19 year old American boy, armed and afraid.

Your date of birth could be the difference between being drafted and sent to Vietnam and being free to choose your life's path. While still a young man I had prepared myself to join the military. I cut through the drama of waiting for a letter to arrive in the mail by volunteering for everything.

I have no idea where I first met Sgt. Paul Maddox. We were both stationed at Ft. Hood Texas in the summer of "67". I don't remember if I met Paul in Texas but I don't think so. Paul and I both requested a transfer to Vietnam about the same time. Paul and I arrived in Hawaii about the same time and were both put in the 11th light infantry brigade's fourth battalion third infantry regiment. We both were assigned to Echo Company of the fourth battalion third infantry regiment which was the heavy weapons company and therefore contained Recon and the four-duce mortars plus other things I am not sure of. I don't think I was aware of sergeant Maddox during this close proximity of duty stations.

Paul Maddox was a veteran Forward Observer. He had completed one tour in Vietnam and was returning for a second tour because that's where the money and rank came fast. Paul had a wife with one in the oven and he needed all the extra pay he could get.

The USS Gordon was about three days west of Hawaii on our scheduled nineteen day trip to Vietnam when I was assigned to KP, kitchen police. Even though there were a couple thousand troops on the USS Gordon I was one of the few that did not get sea sick. I liked KP because it gave me something to do other than watch and smell two thousand sick Army pukes. KP also allowed me to inspect the food closely. I found little black bugs in the bread and wondered if the bugs were the reason my oldest brother told me to join the Army instead of the Navy like he had.

Seven days before we reached Vietnam Echo Company put out a notice that they were looking for someone who would be willing to volunteer as the Forward Observer for Charlie Company fourth battalion third infantry regiment. Apparently the four-duce F.O. assigned to Charlie Company had missed the ship. Someone suggested the AWOL, absent without leave, didn't like the survival odds of an F.O. in combat. I on the other hand was thrilled as the forward observer job was exactly what I wanted. All the other people in the four-duce mortar platoon would spend every day together for the next year sitting on top of a hill. That thought bored me to no end. I wanted to be in the field where things happened. As a four-duce mortar F.O., I would be one of only four people from the heavy weapons section assigned to serve a Company in the field. This whole war thing was coming together real nice for me. I was about to volunteer to become a four-duce F.O. in a war against an Asian opponent.

The platoon leader bid me to enter as soon as I knocked on the hatch of his cabin.

"Sir, I said, I understand you are looking for someone to fill a position as four-duce F.O. and I am here to volunteer". The LT., lieutenant, invited me in to talk about the job.

"Didn't your momma tell you not to volunteer for anything," The Platoon leader said after I had sat down?

"Yes sir, but I won't tell her if you don't", I replied

"What makes you think you can be a forward observer the LT. quizzed?

"Sir, the army trained me in mortars during advanced individual training, AIT, at Ft. Lewis Washington"

The LT. rolled a pencil back and forth on the top of his small desk. "So you're trained but that doesn't answer the question which is, why do YOU want to live outside the wire" he asked?

"Sir", I said," I volunteered for the draft, I volunteered for the infantry and I volunteered for Vietnam so I could find out for myself what war was like. If you force me to stay with the guns on the top of a hill I will go stark raving mad and be a pain in the ass for you. I need to live outside the wire sir because that's where the real war is."

The LT. sat silent for an uncomfortably long period of time rolling his pencil back and forth on his desk top. "OK, you have the job if the senior F.O. clears you. I want you to go to Echo Company and find Sergeant Maddox. You tell him to start a course of training so we can see if you know how to call in a fire mission.

"Yes sir, thank you sir, how do I handle the kitchen police duty sir? I have been put in charge of making sure the little black bugs are equally distributed throughout all the bread on the ship" I responded".

The lieutenant stood up from behind his desk with a smile and said, "You're done with KP, you must have done a good job because every piece of bread I touched had black bugs in it. You go find Sgt. Maddox and start forward observer training ASAP. I will take care of the KP."

"Yes sir, thank you sir," I said while standing at attention and saluting.

Not only was I done with KP but the job held other privileges I was not aware of before I volunteered. The forward observer job was a Sergeant, E-5 position that came with a jeep, a radio and an RTO, radio telephone operator. At the time I was a private E-2 in a Sgt. E-5 slot. The E-5 position exempted me from extra duty unless I was in charge. I would have no more kitchen police nor would I ever have to fill sand bags to build a bunker or burn Diesel soaked human waste in a cut down 50 gallon drum. I could however command a detail filling sandbags or a squad of infantry in combat. The best part of all this was that I would be my own boss. I would be attached to a company in the field but because of my position I would be independent. Things were looking up, my war was coming together.

I found Sgt. Maddox just minutes after being dismissed by the Lieutenant. We agreed to start training first thing in the morning.

I had no more details, no more KP, the rest of my day was clear. I went up on deck for the first time sense going to sea. I smoked a cigarette and let the salty ocean spray wash my childhood away. I was a new man. I felt like the crusader bending on one knee while being knighted by the king. I had approached and opened the door to manhood. Someone else's fear had given me the opportunity to grow.

Sgt. Maddox was a kind and gentle man. He was meticulous in laying out our training plan. He knew his job well and the fact that he had one tour under his belt earned my respect. We trained hard and by day five Sgt. Maddox would start a sentence and I would interrupt him so I could finish the sentence and provide the answer. I knew the material inside and out, the questions and the answers. I could cut corners or do it by the numbers. Sgt. Maddox trained me good. He reported to the platoon leader that I was, "good to go."

Sgt. Maddox and I became friends on the USS General Gordon. We talked about our families and our dreams. I showed him a picture of my girlfriend. It was a black and white photo of her and me standing in the park. Paul offered to add color to the black and white image. I wasn't sure what he had in mind but I gave him the picture and was greatly surprised two days later when he returned my now beautiful picture in living color. I drummed him up a lot of business after that and he was busy until we spotted land.

The USS Gordon docked at Qui Nhon, republic of Vietnam, on December 19, 1967. The privileges kept rolling in my direction. Most people on the ship were ordered to stay on board for one more night while a convoy was organized to take them to Duc Pho, Vietnam, the next day, which was approximately 150 miles north of Qui Nhon.

I was ordered to gather up my gear and the radio telephone operator/driver so we could disembark from the USS Gordon and make sure my jeep was ready for the convoy the next day.

It felt like the light was shining on me because everything was going in my direction. I disembarked the ship with my best friend BW. We were taken to a motor pool that had hundreds of vehicles all painted exactly the same. A motor pool employee tagged us and led us to my jeep. The jeep had a flat tire so I asked the employee about tools, air and patches to fix it. The employee said, "Don't worry about it man, I am a mechanic and I'll take care of everything.

We were free for the day and it was barley after noon. What do two young men do when they find themselves in a war zone with money in their pockets, an M-16 in their hands and the afternoon off? Go to a bar and get drunk is the answer. My first day in Vietnam and I got drunk with my best friend while trying to distinguish between incoming and outgoing artillery rounds. This was too good to make up so it had to be true.

Dec. 20, 1967 the convoy left Qui Nhon and headed for Duc Pho. This was our first exposure to Vietnam and its population. Pre-teen Vietnamese children ran up to our jeep begging for food and/or American citizenship. I was afraid of the children and my imagination allowed them to blow up as they approached our jeep.

"Ok G.I. You like boom-boom my sister, she No. 1 virgin, she love you long time for two dollar" said a twelve year old Vietnamese boy running beside the jeep as it passed his straw hooch on the way to Duc Pho.

On the 23rd of December 1967, four days after arriving in country, Sgt. Maddox walked off the east side of Duc Pho with an ambush from Delta Company. It was after dark. Their mission was to set up an ambush south of our landing zone. I listened on the radio as Sgt Maddox called for an illumination round. Suddenly his radio went dead and word started to filter back that Delta Company had casualties and were returning the ambush to Duc Pho.

I picked up the slack on the radio and continued to adjust illumination rounds. This was my first ever fire mission. Somehow word came to me that Sgt. Maddox had been shot 16 times and was dead. Sgt. Paul Maddox will be the first person in our battalion to die. I was awarded a combat infantry badge for coming under small arms fire while adjusting illumination rounds from a position on the southern slope of Duc Pho.

23 Dec. 67   2140H

Received report from Delta Company that 4.2 F.O. is missing from patrol. Patrol is looking for him. At 2150H Co. D reports SGT Maddox KIA by hostile fire and PFC. Goodwin slightly wounded. Charlie Company requests dustoff, medical evacuation, for four US wounded in action.

Combat Tutorial

A military unit arrives in Theatre or in country and its first task is to acclimate themselves which could take as long as two weeks. As a result we did not do much the first few days on Duc Pho other than play grab ass and practice throwing a bayonet. After we had spent ten days in country the battalion organized a rehearsal combat assault so each company could have the experience of setting up a pick up zone, loading on the choppers, flying to another landing zone, LZ, to conduct search and destroy missions etc. We were the third company to rehearse that day.

Soon after we had boots on the ground I heard a grenade explode and then a hurried cluster of shots fired. I hid, locked and loaded, in a shallow depression with the company commander and his two RTO's, radio telephone operators. I was scared and didn't know which direction I should face in order to freak out. My company commander was a west point graduate with the rank of captain who went to airborne and ranger school before returning for his second tour in Vietnam. If he decided the shallow depression we occupied was adequate cover for the four of us then who was I to argue.

We had lots of chatter and confusion coming over the radio. The lieutenant wanted to know what was happening with his platoon, the captain wanted to know what was happening with his company, the battalion wanted to know who was in charge. I was thinking about getting the hell out of dodge as soon as the shallow depression spit us out.

Two grunts broke through a hedge row prodding a wounded female wearing black pajamas and a surly look on her face. She had been shot in the ass but her defiance overruled the pain. She stood tall and straight in my mind even though she was short and thin in my vision. A grunt pawed at her breast in a fake search wanting to feel if she had tits just because he could.

The captain asked for details about the military age female, MAF, and her two buddies. The grunts said one of her buddies threw a grenade at our 1st squad. The grenade wounded two Americans slightly and the other G.I.'s killed her two friends. She got the bullet in her ass about the same time.

We received the word to pull back and return to base. Somehow I retained custody of the female gook with the spare hole in her body. We were loaded on a chopper and flown back to base.

So this was war. I never saw the two dead males we left at the LZ but I couldn't imagine anyone being tougher than this one; captured, tied up, gagged and shot in the ass female. I had been led to believe that this wounded defiant Vietnamese female was the enemy but I still had no choice but to respect her. She was a little scary, independent, unafraid and capable of going to war with a bullet lodged in her buttocks against heavily armed Americans. She was tougher than the 7.62 full metal jacket round seeded in her ass.

29 Dec. 67   1448H

At 1448H Co C engaged 3-4 VC. One VC threw grenade wounding 2 US. Co C captured 1 female VCS, (Viet Cong suspect) with a bullet in her ass.

With the death of Sergeant Maddox and our contact combat assault rehearsal complete we were prime candidates to go to the bush.

Twenty days after arriving in Vietnam aboard the Merchant vessel USS General Gordon, Charlie Company walked off LZ, landing zone, Doc Pho for its first extended patrol. We would live outside the wire for twenty-eight days, learning to pack our homes on our backs and to see every blade of grass before putting a foot down. We learned how, when and where to dig a foxhole. We were schooled on wearing shorts, petting dogs and checking for scorpions before putting our boots on. We were told that not trimming our toenails could lead to amputation of the foot if you were lucky, implying that more of the leg could be lost if you were not lucky. Being lucky meant a lot to us; it might be all we had, it might be all we needed.

A couple of hours after we walked off Duc Pho we went past a small clump of occupied hooch's. A dog came over to us begging for handouts and a rub behind the ears. He picked the right bunch of young men and was rewarded with food, water and lots of love. Two days later at our NDP, night defensive position, a helicopter brought two medics to our location and announced that anyone who had petted the dog two days earlier would need to receive rabies shots as a precaution. The troops lined up to get their shots in the lower abdomen.

What the troops did not know was that the medics would come to our position every day for the next fourteen days to pump Rabies vaccine into the stomach of every dog loving grunt in the Company. We didn't pet many dogs after that. I lied about touching the animal so I wouldn't have to take shots. I was willing to wait and see if any symptoms appeared.

On the afternoon of our first day's patrol some shots were fired by the point element. I started moving in that direction and by day three outside the wire I was the twelfth man in line. Ten of the eleven first squad members in front of me would be killed or wounded in an explosion and only Zimmerman from first squad will be uninjured.

I carried one pair of extra socks in my rucksack and I wore the rest of my cloths. When they rotted and the jungle ate them a Helicopter would bring us more of the same size fits all. I had ammo, food and gear tucked in various pockets and bandoliers. The PRC-25 radio on my back added 25 pounds to my load. Twenty-five pounds of PRC strapped to my back was a fitting tribute to my humping skills.

My poncho and poncho liner were treasured items. The liner was my bed and the Poncho could be used as a lean to or a pup tent. Several Ponchos fastened together could cover a large area. The two monsoons a year in beautiful Southeast Asia could be met with a single poncho wrapped around the poncho liner that embraced the water soaked and wrinkled dreams of my night.

On one of the darkest nights of this first extended patrol the company had activity with a fire team consisting of between four to six men that had executed a successful ambush. The fire team had made contact and was whispering over the radio for an illumination round so they could measure results or as the grunts would say, get a body count.

I made the illumination fire mission request to the four-duce inch mortar fire direction control, FDC. It pains me to this day to say it took 45 minutes for the Battalion to approve one round of illumination for the ambush with contact. I understand they have many concerns at Battalion. However, I learned this night to say on the radio what they wanted to hear in order to get what

I wanted from them when I wanted it even if what I said was not what I knew to be fact.

The request for illumination was approved around 12:00 PM. The ambush had crawled out in the dark, before the illumination round, and confirmed two dead Vietnamese. The illumination was late and ineffective. The ambush planned to RON, remain over night, their current location and gave us a, wilco, will comply, to a request for a SITREP, situation report, update at first light.

The company had a light step when we moved out from our NDP, night defensive position. This was our first successful ambush and we were anxious to see the grunts that had done it and the gooks they had killed. This is how young men grow to war. They show up and they see for themselves.

As I looked down at the bodies of the two Vietnamese males I felt cold. Their bodies had drained of every day color. They were growing stiff and becoming a bloated shiny blue and purple hue. I didn't want to touch them. I thought that if I touched them their cold would suck the warmth out of my body. Someone started selecting a detail to dig a shallow grave for the two males so I looked busy walking to the river to refill my canteen.

I had filled my canteen at the end of a bend in the river. As I was screwing the lid back on I heard a grunt up-stream say, "Here's another body". I retreated to high ground and walked over to see what he had found. The grunt and another dude were dragging a dead military age female, MAF, out of the water. She had been killed the night before by the same claymore mine blast that had killed her two male friends.

She had lain on her back in the water after dying. Her arms and legs had floated up and frozen in that position. She had advanced rigor mortis.

It dawned on me that I had filled my canteen downstream from her dead decaying body. Did you feel the shiver that just went through your spine and that kind of chill sound that came out of your mouth, that's what I had?

Do they call it cannibalism when you make tea out of a dead body because that's what I had in my canteen? I had dead person tea. I felt a shiver and jive run up my spine, pour that shit out, run up stream and rinse my canteen until someone makes me stop. I don't want any rigor mortis tea. I don't need any rigor mortis tea.

The company started moving out but I hung around with the burial detail. We bitched and moaned about having to scrap two shallow graves as we dragged the Vietnamese males into each without much fanfare. At least the males were flat. They were covered up in a few minutes and looked like they might stay there awhile.

The female was a different matter. How do we bury her with her arms and legs sticking up like that? Someone said we should cut her up into pieces. The silence that followed that statement eliminated the need to debate the suggestion. Someone else suggested we roll her on her side. The rigor mortis had set in with her legs spread and knees bent. Any way we rolled her the depth of the hole we were preparing was shy of what was needed to cover the body. We could have dug deeper but no one suggested that because we were already taking on water in the grave.

We placed her into the shallow grave without much respect. One guy tried to stand on her arm to push it down but that jacked the other side of her body up into the air so someone else had to put a foot on her torso to force that part down. This was not pretty. We were a crude and inexperienced burial detail.

She kept sticking out of the hole like a whack-a-moll. It's like she didn't want to be buried but we kept pushing her back into the ground. The rest of us attempted to cover the body with all the available lose dirt.

Because there is a God I am sure that shortly after we left the grave site the Vietnamese female's arm popped out of the dirt. And because God laughs in colors, all her fingers would be curled inward touching the palm except the middle one and it would be flipping off the entire planet. A ghostly female voice could be heard to drift across the fog draped rice paddy saying, "You fucked up my whole day asshole". If they ever build a road here I am sure the Audubon society will drive by and comment, "Oh look, a pretty bird sticking out of the ground".

I called the targets fast walkers. If they ran we would shoot them. Fast walkers took rapid short steps so they could move fast without looking like they were running. Sometimes we would let the fast walkers go because maybe they had an appointment with a water Buffalo or we didn't feel like shooting. Fast walkers are Vietnamese who don't want to be killed. If they ran we would shoot them.

I was traveling with a five man fire team of fourth Battalion grunts. We were on a circular kind of patrol designed to last the afternoon and take a look at the surrounding area. We had worked our way up a hill to a ridge which ran north/northeast to a taller hill some 500 meters distant. The vegetation at our current spot was uncommonly short so we stopped to take a break and scan the area. The PRC-25 radio on my back squawked to life.

"Foxtrot, this is Charlie 4/1 over".

"Go 4/1".

"Roger, is that you on the ridge, over?"

"That's a most affirmative roger, over".

"We have 2 gooks *đi nhanh,* go fast, from our location. Can you engage, over?"

I responded on the radio, "Will comply, out".

The distance from us to the fast walkers on the rice patty dike may have been 600 meters. The drop in elevation was more than 100 feet. The fast walkers were big time *i nhanh* go fast. Our M-60 gunner began putting 7.62 rounds down range. Its real tough to fire offhand with an M-60, the weapon weighs 23.15 pounds and the ammo is a killer whether carried inside or outside the body. The gunner tried three or four bursts with negative results. Another grunt in our patrol said, "Let me try". This guy brings his M-16 up, fires one round and I see one of the fast walkers drop off the rice paddy dike. The shooter fires a couple rounds toward the second fast walker with negative results. We gathered up our gear and headed down the hill. The radio cracked to life again.

"Foxtrot, this is 4/1, over"

"Go 4/1"

"We have confirmed your kill. One VC, Vietnamese communist, KIA, killed in action, no weapon, good shooting out."

It took us 20 minutes to work our way to the kill. I jumped off the rice paddy dike and looked real close at the body in an attempt to locate the entry hole. I could see where his right ear had been cut off with a knife shortly before. I rolled the gook over to view his other side. The KIA, killed in action, had a bullet hole in the middle of his left ear. That is amazing I thought, 600 meters down range, over 100 feet down slope on a moving target. This has to be the best shot I have ever seen in my life.

When we rejoined the rest of the company a dude from the confirming patrol offered to give me the gooks ear as a trophy. He said it was my kill and I had the option of claiming the ear. The E-5 leader of my patrol also told me 30 years later that in an email that the kill belonged to me. I want to think I never killed anyone while in Vietnam. I didn't want the trophy ear. I would not take ownership for the kill. Within a week of collecting ears or fingers from the dead the flesh generally turns black and shriveled. The grunt, who removed the ear from a dead body, will use the body part as a necklace or drop it in the hand of a F.N.G., fucking new guy, to impress or freak them out. All that aside, this was still the best shot I have ever seen regardless of who made it.

I still claim that I never killed anyone while in Vietnam. I took some shots at people and a couple of them dropped out of sight but I never confirmed the kill. I did however save the life of an eight year old girl once by requesting a dust off. I also saved the life of a thirty year old Vietnamese man by putting myself between him and the six or so grunts that were shooting at him. It turned out that the gook was a card carrying patriot who didn't need to be killed. I didn't need to kill to become a man. I came to Vietnam to learn about life and war and death. If I needed to kill to protect my friends or myself I think I would have but who knows. Until it happens, who knows?

Watching

I watched them come in numbers both large and small
Anxious, with bright eyes and
A lightning fast trigger finger
Never used
Amputated in the explosion that transforms
A grunt into a hero
I watched them come and now I remember forever
Those days

Seven days in April

Every day sense the year 2000 I have carried a list of dates and names carefully folded three times and placed with a lighted candle in the church of my mind. The words are written in code and can only be translated by mixing blood and pain. When my clothes are tattered remnants and the soles of my boots are held together with shoe strings the coded words flow from the lips of the dead begging, remember me.

Remembering their names is difficult when you never knew them when you knew them. We had nick names, not real ones.

Zimmerman was the eleventh man in line when a bouncing Betty wounded or killed the other ten people in his squad. I was standing behind Zimmerman and we were tasked to walk that line. I didn't know their names. On April 19, 1968 I was positioned behind Zimmerman when my friend John-John died from an explosion and I didn't know anyone's name. Not even John-John's. I would not know their names for over 30 years.

APRIL 19, 1968

At 0856 hours, C Company request dustoff ,medical evacuation, for 3 U.S. WHA, wounded hostile action, due to detonation of booby trapped AP, anti-personal mine vicinity of BS533853, dustoff completed 0902 hrs. 1 other U.S. KHA, Killed hostile action, Pers. concerned: SP4 Pennamon KHA, 2nd Lt. O'Neil-WHA, PFC Hargrove-WHA, and Finn-WHA. Note, PFC Hargrove's wounds will also prove to be fatal.

APRIL 20, 1968

At 1623 hrs 3d plat Company C received 20 rounds of small arms sniper fire from vic. BS503878. Fire was returned with negative results.

APRIL 21, 1968

At 1240 hrs C Company requests dust-off for 1 VN,Vietnamese, female w/unknown illness in the vicinity of grid BS510852, Medevac completed 1300 hrs.

At 1560 hrs 1st plat Company C rec. 6-8 rounds. AW, automatic weapons, fire, believed to be AK-47 vic. BS503877; search conducted after contact was broken w/neg. results.

On April 22, Zimmerman and I will drop to our stomachs and crawl over to Sgt. Fox who received a bullet in his stomach after it had passed through his M-16 collecting steel and plastic it will deposit inside his body. I didn't know Sgt. Fox or Zimmerman's names at the time; I didn't need to know their names while I lay on the ground talking on the radio to the dust-off pilot and the helicopter gunship flying cover.

Thirty-three years later, five days before 911, I dropped to my stomach on a driveway in North Carolina as Sgt. Don Fox came out of his house to greet me. We knew each other's name then and dropping to my stomach was a staged reenactment I had planned for months to help remind us of the last time we had seen each other; on our bellies, seeking a shadow to hide behind, just before the dustoff chopper arrived.

APRIL 22, 1968

At 0715 hrs, CO C, grid, BS504875, request dustoff: 1 US; litter; stomach wound; urgent. Medevac completed 0724 hrs. Details of the injury will follow.

At 0715 hrs 1st plat Company C rec. five to six bursts of AW fire from vic. BS507878 resulting in I U.S. WHA, Sgt., sergeant, Fox.

At 0920 hrs Company C req. dustoff; 1 US litter patient; urgent; nature of injury, booby trap. Medevac completed 0932 hrs. Remarks: 1 US WHA, Sgt. Richard Cooper. 1 U.S. KHA, killed hostile action, PFC. Michael Price.

At 1516 hours Company C requests a dustoff for 1 VN with lockjaw.

On April 22, 1968 I will see the APC, run over a land mine. This will be the one and only time I will have this experience in Vietnam. We were set up perhaps 40 yards away watching the track when it hit the mine while trying to flush out a sniper. Our mission was to move for three days and cordon off an area we called sniper alley. Delta Company would share in the joy and move for several days also before joining us at the sniper alley cordon convention center. When the cordon was complete we put on gas masks and dropped CS gas from the four-duce mortars into the center and waited for the sniper to run out with his hands up.

The problem was that the sniper was probably deep in a hole; he had been shooting at every company that passed through the area for about four months, thus the name, "Sniper Alley". The CS gas was being delivered above ground. Gas is light so it goes up and it cannot fall in a hole. We were losing a lot of people to do this mission and so was Delta Company. I never did see the sniper but I think I heard someone laugh and it wasn't us.

At 1542 hrs, 2d platoon of E Troop ran over and detonated land mine Vic. BS523887 Unknown size mine, resulting in no casualties and blown track on M113 APC, armored personal carrier. The crew is presently performing repairs on M113 track.

On April 23 I will call in a dustoff and help police up the body parts plus equipment from a booby trap placed in a hedgerow. I will not know their names.

APRIL 23, 1968

At 1405 Company C requests a dustoff for 2 U.S. WHA from detonating Bouncing Betty anti-personnel mine. The medevac was completed at 1420 hours.

At 1511 Co. C. requested a dustoff for 2 US KHA Vic. BS 527853, resulting from detonation of M16 AP mine. Lewis Harmon, KHA, Russell Matheny, KHA.

APRIL 24, 1968

At 1836 Co. C. requested a dustoff grid BS535801Tripped boo-by trap resulting in 3 U.S. WHA; wounded hostile action, Pfc. John Pollite, Pvt. Thomas Brzoska Pvt. Payton Leslie. Medevac completed at1850.

On April 25th I called in a dustoff for Zimmerman and three others. I remembered Zimmerman's name this time because he departed as a psychological casualty. I thought him so brave because he knew when he had seen enough war. His squad had been wiped out twice in our first four months in country. He was the only survivor and he had become their pain. I remembered his name but I have never seen him sense that day. Even though he does not know who I am I search for him often.

APRIL 25, 1968

At 1520 Company C. request dustoff in the vicinity BS533798. Result of M16A1 AP mine. Pfc. Eric Fickland, KHA. SP4 George Jacobs, KHA, Pfc. Zimmerman, WHA. George Daise, WHA.

When we came off the April patrol Charlie Company occupied a hill inside the wire with sandbag bunkers and less strenuous activities but still including short patrols, ambushes and perimeter security.

A chopper chaplain flew into the firebase on a helicopter and set up a prayer center. He held a nondenominational service for the dead. I am sure his visit brought comfort to some of the dozen or so grunts from Charlie Company who attended the service. I was one of the zombies who were not seeking comfort. I wanted truth.

Shirtless, wearing web gear including pistol belt, first aid kit, ammo pouches and a canteen, the angry outrider in me began circling 90 feet from the groups centre. I would sometimes stop and squat, just like the Asians who have never seen a chair, cradling an M-16 in my arms and hosting a steel pot on my head. My anger was demanding truth. I was chain smoking hot boxed cigarettes and leaving behind a cloud that drifted perfectly with the chopper chaplain's incense. My smoke was bitter and aggressive while the chaplain's incense burnt transparent odors that became whimsical and fading in my soul.

The chaplain didn't know the names of our dead and wounded or how they had died. He didn't know how they had died. The outrider, tracked by the Chaplin's eyes as if he had been pre-warned about the possibility of encountering people like me, circled the group like a vulture poised to swoop in at the earliest opportunity with the word truth, flying on my wings.

The spirits about me evoked a silent scream; "they didn't need to die, not for the chopper Chaplain, not for God and not for the country. They didn't need to die". I would speak from my heart to the ones who rally in support of corporate sponsored blood and the profits on their ledgers. I do not carry the supporter's names in a sacred place; written in code and folded three times.

Days ran into weeks and my known location on the planet was restricted to the size of the plastic covered 1:50,000 scale military map I folded four times and stuck into the side pocket of my olive drab pants. Beyond the edges of the 1:50,000 military maps there might be nothing. The next step could find me falling off the edge of the earth. The next explosion might change everything. We seldom see the enemy so we turn the things we do see into the enemy. Sometimes, our rage was spent on hooch's and even a slow moving animal would be punished. You know what they say; "If you can't shoot the one you love then shoot the one you're with".

The company had moved into a RON, remain over night, position. It was about 1830 hours. We were digging in, erecting shelters, opening C rations, drying socks and airing our feet out. A grunt 40 feet to my west on the bank of a deep, narrow, slow moving river alerted to a canoe holding two Vietnamese males. I grabbed my M-16 and moved to the river bank with three to six others. There was at least one officer in this group. I heard someone hail the two MAM's, military age males. The Vietnamese did not respond. One of the American grunts put some M-16 rounds in the water close to the canoe. The MAM's started waving their arms above their heads while shouting to the G.I.'s in broken English; "me no VC, me no VC, GI number one, VC number fucking ten".

I heard someone in the group quietly say, Light them up! A grunt with an M-60 machine gun put some serious rounds down range. The military age male sitting in the canoe toppled over backwards from the impact of multiple 7.62 rounds screaming through his body. He plunged backward awkwardly into the slow dark water beneath the canoe.

The gunner continued to spit hot lead at the military age male standing upright. The MAM was dead and wanted to fall forward to join his friend in the water but the rounds from the M-60 were impacting his upper body with such force that he could not fall forward. He was dead, standing, dancing like a Marionette on the end of a puppeteer's string. When the M-60 gunner stopped firing the MAM acted like a giant slinky. Dead bodies have no muscle control, none. The MAM slinky melted to the bottom of the canoe and then gracefully slinked over the wooden side of the boat and entered the water with little or no splash.

One of the grunts in the group stripped and dived into the water to retrieve the MAM's bodies. He located them one at a time and floated the remains to the bank where several sets of willing hands removed the MAM's from the water. Upon searching the bodies we discovered that both MAM's had proper I.D.'s. The

I.D.'s were issued by the South Vietnamese government as a sign that the card carrier was loyal to the Saigon regime. We destroyed the I.D.'s and reported to Battalion, two VC, KIA, killed in action, one canoe destroyed, no weapons, out.

Shoot 'em

The nights in Vietnam always brought on the greatest amount of fear. We would lie alone on the ground after dark surrounded by deadly silence. Late at night, the suffocating heat of the Southeast Asian day would have spent its dynamic impact. A chill, ever so slight yet compelling in its contrast to the exhausting daytime standards, would touch our bodies.

I know the whisper of fear that lies on the belly of a grunt during ambush. A grunt alone in the dark feels the haunting chill of the early morning dew, which sinks deep inside the wounded soul, cold and alone.

There was a time during my tour in 1968 when I knew I was crazy. I had practically died from the pain of seeing the broken and grotesquely mutilated bodies of the members of Charlie Company. Sometimes I walked point, looking for death, several days in a row. For a while I went on an ambush every other night. This was an act of suicide and murder. Suicide for myself and murder for anyone around me because of the danger my actions presented. I remember the details but not the time or place of these ambushes. The memories are made up of disturbing cloudy visions surrounded by doubt and fear.

This day was just like a hundred days before and a hundred days that would follow. The company began to stir at first light. The SITREP (situation report) coming over the PRC-25 radio became more audible. The voices on the other end of the radio gained volume in lockstep with the increasing daylight. The louder voices were a good sign. We could sense and hear other people thus rendering our lonely chill tame. With the sounds and sights of others, we were not so alone.

From my position with the command group in the center of our perimeter, I could watch the platoons and squads go through their morning rituals. Someone over there was brushing his teeth; another grunt was heating water in a canteen cup with C-4 so he could mix powdered hot chocolate or foul-tasting powered coffee. The more the morning light burned away the gentle dew, the greater the activity within the company. We regained confidence each morning.

I could see grunts filling in a foxhole or putting on dry socks; another grunt was putting away his shaving gear or rolling up his poncho and repacking his rucksack. An officer would stop by to get his marching orders for the day from the company commander. A platoon sergeant or medic would report blisters, infection, and cases of FUO (fever of unknown origin) for their men. The greater activity saw the men picking up the claymore mines and trip flares in front of their positions. A squawk on the radio would indicate the ambush announcing their intent to reenter the perimeter.

We lived under the same clothes, day and night, until they were eaten away by the jungle or dissolved in the toxic waste of the rice patties. I wore out five pairs of boots in the ten months I humped with Charlie Company. I had the option of traveling with the command group, who could follow two platoons through the jungle after a trail had been established. The grunts in the lead had to fight through the vegetation while every vine ripped and grabbed their clothes and boots. It is possible the grunts on point were wearing out a pair of boots a month. The jungle surrounds, kills, and eats everything. We would sweat bucket loads each day, and I once went six weeks between showers."Other army units and combat marines had it much worse than we did.

With the daylight fully established and the previous night's application of mosquito repellent beginning to cause swelling on my face, the commanding officer would order, seemingly without words or motion, "Ruck- up, gentlemen. Move out."

Many times we would move in two columns. Once we arrived at the new location, the platoons would range out and sweep the surrounding area. Other times we would fan out and sweep a large area while moving toward a new NDP (night defensive position). On this particular day, we moved in two columns. During the movement one of the platoons identified and registered a good ambush position for that night.

Around 1600 the entire company moved into a new NDP. We dug foxholes and put up shelters made of ponchos. I registered four-deuce mortars around our location for reference. I had learned to use illumination as my first round when registering any kind of fire. Illumination was a safe round and gave me a good idea of where other types of ordinance would land should I need it later.

The company hung up their socks to dry and took off their sweat-soaked shirts in an attempt to air them out. White streaks of salt-laden sweat stained our shoulders and backs. Some shirts were so filled with these salty stains that when they dried they could stand up without support. Grunts opened up C rats and performed their individual magic to construct a meal. To all on looking eyes, we appeared to be preparing to spend the night in this location.

Around 2200 hours the entire company silently strapped on our gear and moved out. I attached myself to a four-person fire team with a mission to set up an ambush in the spot that had been chosen earlier. I hooked up with this team under the pretense that my radio could be used to call for fire if needed. That was true, but the real reason was simply to give a grunt a break by allowing him to stay with the company and possibly get one extra hour of sleep. The grunts needed any break they could get.

We set up the ambush along a well-used trail. The night moved to dawn without incident. About 0630 the E-5 in charge of the unit gave the word to gather our gear and retrieve claymores so we could move out. About thirty seconds later, one of the grunts alerted us to a gook on the trail. I looked up and saw an unarmed forty-year-old male who looked to me like he was headed out to farm.

The E-5 in charge of the ambush belted out loudly, "Shoot 'em!"

I turned to face the sergeant and said, "He's a farmer, man. He doesn't even have a fucking weapon, man."

The E-5 had been standing to my left rear. He took several steps forward, which put him at my right front, and placed his back toward me. As he walked past, I could taste the hate in his eyes. I had challenged his judgment, and he was the designated god on this ambush. He once again loudly ordered a grunt to shoot the gook.

A grunt with an M79 fired his buckshot-filled round at a human target not more than fifteen feet away. The M79 holds a 40x46 mm round that allows large volumes of discharge material.

I swear to this day that I saw sparks fly off the farmer's chest and forehead as the buckshot picked him up and deposited him on his back in the middle of the trail. His arms and legs went spastic like someone exposed to a nerve agent. He was break dancing before it had been invented. He was a trendsetter.

Another grunt pulled out his .45 to finish off the local. His first shot hit the local in the leg. The grunt stepped closer and fired a second round, which hit the farmer in the arm. The grunt stepped even closer and put a round in the guy's chest that either scared him to death or found a sweet spot. Either way, he died.

We rolled the body off the trail and finished preparing our rucksacks for the move to rejoin the company. Later we called the Company CO on the PRC-25 and reported: one VC KIA (killed in action), no weapon, out. It would take me more than twenty years to talk about this incident.

Some days we walked to work and some days we flew. On this occasion we executed a combat assault by helicopter into the Task Force Barker area of operation. We called the area "Pinksville," and history would later come to call it "My Lai." Lt. Calley was convicted of war crimes committed while serving in Task Force Barker on March 16, 1968.

Charlie Company 4/3 and I were nineteen klicks—19,000 meters, or about twelve miles—to the west-northwest of the Task Force Barker area of operation when Charlie Company 1/20 was burning the hooch's in My Lai. I believe my company did three different assaults into the My Lai area during 1968. A belief is not a reality in war. It is rather a hunch fortified by a notion that is reinforced in dreams that haunt the nights of a grunt.

The LZ (landing zone) was cold, and all lifts landed without incident on the palm-tree-studded white sandy beach. I attached myself to a platoon that was tasked to form a line and sweep the area. Soon after we moved out, I was approached by a military-age female who was packing an eight-year-old girl with a bullet lodged high in her right cheek. I called a medic over to have him look at the wound. He confirmed that the bullet had been in the little girl's face for several days and that we should call a dustoff, a medical evacuation helicopter. The medic left to work on a grunt's foot as I led the adult female and child over to the lieutenant in command of the platoon. I asked him if he would call in a dustoff for the little girl.

The lieutenant went ballistic on me and started acting like a punk. He was a bigmouthed tough guy who had transformed from a highly trained military leader into a limp prick. This dude was over his head in a command position. I had met the perfect officer-asshole combination. "Every fucking one of them is out after dark planting booby traps to kill us, and then they want our help in the daytime," the lieutenant ranted. "Fuck them, fuck their children, and fuck the water buffalo they rode in on. If they ain't gooks, then they work for the fucking gooks."

I must make this clear: the small unit infantry commander is one of the most challenging positions on this planet. By "small units" I speak of platoon- and company-size infantry units. Anything above the company level and you become disconnected from the fight. A colonel may direct the battle from a command and control chopper a thousand feet off the ground, but he is disconnected from the battle whether he knows it or not. He may see more than the grunts on the ground, but he cannot feel the battle's pain, and without the pain his decisions become uninformed.

A platoon might consist of thirty-two soldiers on the parade ground. That number is cut almost in half as soon as they deploy. A company of light infantry with a full complement of medics, forward observers, headquarters personnel, etc., might total 182 people inside the wire. Once we would cross the wire and get boots on the ground, the company would quickly shrink in strength to about a hundred people.

The officer in charge of these undermanned small units must look after every detail for their men. They cannot afford to lose anyone. The smallest blister is no less important than the radio frequency of available artillery and helicopter gunships. An officer must make decisions that may result in the death of his men. Like Gen. Robert E. Lee said to Gen. Stewart at the Battle of Gettysburg, officers must love the army but be willing to order the death of the thing they love.

The platoon commander chooses the squad to achieve a mission knowing full well that the deaths will not go quietly by his soul. He may have pretense as a master of his own heart, but time and circumstance see the truth of his confidence. He must know the depth of his charge's pain; the limits already reached, and ask still again for more spirit to reach even further. He must break them before sharing their sorrows. He must lead them to, through, and out of the pain.

These leaders also have access to an awesome display of weapons that have but one purpose: to destroy all they touch. Sometimes, and now more than ever, civilians are thrown into the mix to suffer. We could have contests to see who suffers the most. There would be many winners.

The officer throwing a fit in front of me was not handling the situation well. He could have used a lollipop. He had the right and the authority, plus a heavily armed platoon, to do whatever he ordered. I had a PRC-25 radio and the frequency of the commanding officer.

Did I mention that I helped dig the command position foxhole most nights? If I wasn't on ambush, I would share the command group fighting position. Not only shared but helped to construct. I would also pull radio watch collecting SITREPs from the squads, ambushes, and platoons and then issuing a combined company SITREP to higher-higher at the battalion level during my nighttime shift. When we did everything right, the captain got lots of needed sleep, which made the whole company better. I got along good with Capt. Sam. His rank and my radio would win this pissing contest with an out-of-tune officer.

The company commander's call sign was always "Charlie six," which we shortened to "six" after we made contact. His RTO's call sign was "Charlie six-alpha." My call sign was "Charlie Foxtrot Oscar," which stood for Charlie Company Forward Observer; my handle quickly became "Foxtrot."

"Six, this is Foxtrot, over."

"Six-alpha, go Foxtrot, over."

"Roger, six-alpha, request dustoff for one local preteen female with bullet lodged high up in her right cheek, my location, my smoke, how copy, over."

"Wait-one, out."

"Foxtrot, this is six-alpha, over."

"Go six-alpha, over."

"Six wants to know if the medic gives the wound an emergency status, over."

"That's a most affirmative, Roger, over."

"Permission granted. The dustoff on the way, switch to their frequency, over and out."

I watched the military-age female and her wounded daughter load into the dustoff chopper and fly away.

Is there a secret place where we learn to hate and fear an eight-year-old girl with a bullet lodged high up in her right cheek? Is this just another secret hate/fear thing related to war? Why are there so many secrets about war? Why do we not talk about the things we have seen and done? Why do civilians buy flags and send others to war only to turn their backs and not listen to the stories after we have returned? Maybe part of my task is to examine some of the secrets.

Combat Jack

In the city of Mogadishu and the country of Somalia, they called it "combat jack." I am talking about the Delta Force teams and 75th Army Rangers in the movie *Black Hawk Down*. Combat jack is one of the secrets about war asking for my attention.

Considering all of the events that had taken place, I had no expectation of receiving even one extra minute of life; the future was simply my next step accompanied by an explosion. Because I had already died inside, it made perfect sense to me to begin walking point several days in a row and going on ambush in the night. I was an FO attached to the command group. Whenever the CO told a platoon they would be on point, I would hook up with them and they were happy to let me up front. When the company CO called a platoon leader over to coordinate an ambush, I would volunteer to go along and assist the ambush with my PRC-25 radio. I do not remember ever having a unit refuse to let me join them.

On one occasion I volunteered to man the clacker while on ambush. A clacker is a palm-size plastic electric generator approximately six inches long by four inches high by one inch thick. The top of the clacker has a hinged plastic handle that can generate a two-volt charge when squeezed hard. The clacker is connected to a claymore mine by a fifty-foot length of wire. The claymore will explode when the clacker sends a charge of electricity down the wire to a blasting cap inserted into the mine. The back blast from the claymore can be as deadly as the steel balls coming out the front.

A claymore mine is a convex piece of plastic approximately ten inches long, six inches high, and two inches thick with folding metal legs on the bottom. The inside of the claymore is filled with one pound of C-4 explosive and hundreds of little steel balls. In military terms the claymore mine is a command detonated directional antipersonnel mine. The claymore is a preferred weapon for ambush patrols and perimeter defense.

Establishing and maintaining an ambush is an eerie prospect at best. Sometimes we would move into position after dark. The ambush leader would assign positions to each grunt with a weapon. Sometimes the ambush leader would call for a 50 percent alert, which meant that every two hours half of the ambush would wake up and relieve the other half. If the ambush made contact, everyone would wake up soon enough to dispatch his assigned load, which usually consisted of one magazine of M16 and one grenade. The grenade would not be thrown if the ambush was surrounded by trees, because a grenade could bounce off a tree and land in your own lap.

Some ambushes required 100 percent alert based on the tactical situation or the ambush leader's decision. The maximum alert ambush patrols were extremely difficult for the grunts. They were required to hump all day, lay on the cold ground fighting fatigue to stay awake while clutching powerful weapons all night, and then hump excessive loads through difficult terrain and balls-burning humidity all the next day. They learned to catch a night's worth of sleep during a fifteen-minute break under a scorching hot sun.

Civilians rarely understand the implications of an ambush patrol. How do you go to the bathroom when on ambush or while marching during the day? The answer is that you piss your pants.

You piss your pants the first time because the situation demands it. Any motion or noise is unacceptable on an ambush. To stand up and drop your pants could get you shot by your own people. You piss your pants the second or third time without much thought. It is funny to think that our parents spend a great deal of time potty training us and then, when we seek to become men who kill and die, we resort to pissing our pants out of necessity.

Most young men—and at age twenty-one I was a young man—have a perpetual erection. It is a scientific fact that every time a male dreams it is accompanied by an erection. The blood lust experienced by some in combat has a sexual element to it. This is not new information. During the Crusades the armies routinely raped the women of their enemies. During the Second Sino-Japanese War, the Japanese systematically raped and murdered thousands in what is known as the "Rape of Nanking."

A good Facebook friend I have never met in person was a Vietnam combat medic with the 1/7 Cavalry in 1970. When I quizzed him about jacking off in combat he said that a friend in Echo Company's Recon Platoon of the 2/5 Cavalry once told him that he was so turned on after a patrol that he went behind a tree and jacked off. The 1/7 combat veteran suggested that sex and violence have been connected throughout history.

I asked another friend about this subject, and he said he had masturbated during a combat patrol. "I too did jack," he said. "Sometimes the never-ending presence of death and fear demanded some release. It was a desperate, almost futile attempt to find small moments of pleasure in what would otherwise be endless agonizing days of hell."

Another friend I have never met in person said that during one of his two tours in Afghanistan he had jacked off after experiencing combat. He said in a humorous Australian outback accent, "the combat jack. 'Oi, I had a wank-break whilst in the Du-auzy bowl between fire-missions while covering the 120 millimeter mortar crew!"

In the book *Black Hawk Down*, a by-the-numbers but inexperienced army ranger, with his hair high and tight and his weapons plus equipment up to code, has a conversation with a Delta Force veteran who has long hair, practices unorthodox weapons procedures, never salutes, and dresses like the natives. These two combat troops have a one-paragraph discussion about what is called the "combat jack." In the movie *Black Hawk Down*, this conversation is reduced to one short sentence; you will know you're a combat veteran when the danger-filled tension of war demands release and sex or jacking off is the way home.

Another well-respected twenty-year friend who served with the 173rd Airborne Brigade for thirty months in Vietnam has his own story. This highly experienced combat veteran told me of his trials with the bloodlust after escaping from a four foot by four foot bamboo prison that resembled a tiger cage. As a sergeant he would not return his LRRP (long-range recon patrol) team from patrol unless he had blood on his hands and clothes. On one occasion he was forced to kill a chicken to maintain his bloodlust oath. On another occasion he used his jungle knife to cut the fetus out of a live pregnant female. He strapped a block of C-4 plastic explosive and a grenade to the fetus and dropped it in a well. He said he creamed his pants while engaged in this terrible act. He climaxed sexually while killing a woman and child. Because of the unacceptable trauma related to this act, the LRRP, guilt ridden, is still committing slow suicide by consuming Jack and smack daily.

On this particular ambush, late at night, I had the clacker in my hand while I humped the ground. I experienced sexual arousal and became confused and guilt ridden. This secret would stay in my heart for over thirty years before I read the book and saw the movie *Black Hawk Down*. The next morning after the ambush, I knew I was done with war. I had seen and done too much. I still gave all I had, but I didn't have much left to give. I had become a liability; I was fucked up. As we humped to rejoin the company the next morning, the ambush leader asked me what was wrong. I couldn't put it into words. That would take another forty years.

The combat jack may be the point at which I went from FU (fucked up) to FUBAR (fucked up beyond all recognition). It was the combat jack that convinced me I had been in country long enough to leave country and go home. But it had to be an honest departure. No shuck and jive, either dead or alive.

I have another personal account I want to share with you. This story bothers me a great deal, and I hope that I can relate the events in such a way that you are bothered too. You must show up if you want to go there.

It was a beautiful, hot, cloudless Southeast Asian day sometime in 1968. Our company was conducting a search and destroy mission ten to twenty miles southwest of Chu Lai. We were operating between the South China Sea and the jungle-covered mountains to our west. The command group for the company had established a moving CP (command post) on a well-used high-speed trail wide enough for water-buffalo-pulled carts to pass each other.

The designated maneuver platoons and squads were ranging out to the east and west following smaller trails that led to isolated single hooch's or groups of hooch's. As we moved south, a growing column of smoke became visible as if to tell Charlie, "We have Zippo lighters and we be burning your home and killing your livestock." Charlie could determine our direction and rate of March simply by watching the column of smoke. We were like bullies who taunt the enemy and who act surprised when the enemy comes and kicks our ass. We say things like, "did they know we were here?"

I hooked up with three FNGs (fucking new guys) from a first squad fire team. They were from the cursed squad that had been wiped out twice during our first four months in country. We followed a small partially overgrown trail leading to the northeast. The trail worked itself through and around several hedgerows and came to a dead end at a man-made clearing approximately fifty yards in diameter. The clearing contained one hooch, two adults, a working garden, and some small farm animals in the form of pigs and chickens.

I had been trailing the three grunts and, as we entered the opening, moved to a position on the left flank. I took the safety off of my M16 and brushed my finger against the trigger housing while taking a very close look at the surrounding vegetation. We were on the edge of a clearing that was hemmed in by thick brush and tall trees. This was a great kill zone for Charlie as soon as we stepped out of the brush, and a real dumb place for us to be. I was on high alert and ready to go to ground at the first metallic sound or gunshot. By this point in my tour, I had perfected the art of concealing my entire body behind a blade of grass. I had done it before when I saw a .51 caliber round kick up dirt close to a blade of grass that I would eventually propose to. Being hit by a .51 caliber round near the horseshoe on the south side of the *Song Tra Khuc* was not my idea of a good day. Having a blade of grass that I planned to wed shield my ass was a great day.

Out of the corner of my right eye, I detected movement coming from the doorway of the hooch. I heard one of the grunts say, "Let's rape her." Before those words fully registered, another grunt said, "Yeah, let's do it, man." I did not understand what was happening. We were Americans; we were not supposed to do this shit. I didn't know what to do. I had momma and poppa gook under the gun. They had not yet been searched or bound.

The young female kept walking out of the hooch and toward the two adults in the clearing. The adults may have been her parents or grandparents, I don't know, but things were going south way too fast.

All three grunts grabbed the Vietnamese chick and began dragging her into the hooch. I didn't know what to do. I thought about busting off some rounds, but I figured the grunts would cut the girl's throat and kill the two adults. I was confused about what to do and needed help to find the answer. I looked intently at the surrounding vegetation and hoped that Charlie was in the bushes. I wished he would kill me and the three grunts because what we were doing was wrong.

There is a good chance that I would not have fired back. Charlie also had a job to do, and we deserved to die. My eyes drifted back to the faces of the two adults. I was silently mouthing, "Fuck me." I lowered the barrel of my M16 and tried to give the adults an opportunity to i *nhanh* (go fast). They stood frozen fast, defiant. I switched the safety on my M16 to the on position and moved my finger to the side of the trigger housing.

Thoughts about killing the Americans began to pass through my mind. Things had gone so far south that I had circled the planet. Fuck me. I was working on a plan to kill the grunts when one of them came out the door of the hooch holding up his pants with one hand and managing his M16 with the other. I couldn't work out the plan in my head about what to do. If I killed the grunts, I knew I would spend the rest of my life in prison.

A few minutes later, the second grunt came out of the hooch. He was pulling up his pants and fastening his belt. I began to believe God would take care of things. God would blow their sorry-ass legs off tomorrow with a Bouncing Betty. God would have them die of a sucking chest wound where all they could do was lie on their backs in the mud and listen to their lives fade away one gurgling, bubbling, wheezing sucking chest wound sound after the other.

The third grunt came out of the hooch. I did not see a knife or blood on his hands. I thought a one-word prayer that at least they did not kill her. It is possible the only reason they left her alive was to save her for me.

One of the grunts looked at me and said, "It's your turn, man."

A second grunt chimed in, "Yeah, man. We got her warmed up for you. Hahaha."

I moved the barrel of my weapon from the adult gooks to a spot on the ground between me and the three grunts. I returned the safety to the off position and gently rested my finger on the trigger. I think I was ready for a gunfight. If they had moved a muscle in my direction, I believe I would have responded properly. I hope, I wish, I don't know.

I heard mama-san and papa-san wailing as they ran toward the hooch holding their loved one. My God, I thought. What have we done? The three grunts were smiling and cracking jokes.

I was hoping that at the very least God would fill these three grunts with a lifetime of guilt and shame and remorse. I don't think God listens to me on these kinds of matters. We began moving back up the trail to the west. I positioned myself last. The safety was off and my finger was heavy on the trigger. The Vietnamese behind me was less of a threat than the Americans I was following.

About fifty yards up the trail at a bend that turned us slightly to the south stood a small private pagoda. The three grunts stopped long enough to light the pagoda on fire. To put this into perspective, it would be like going to your neighbor's house, raping their daughter, and then burning their church. From my point of view, God was on vacation this day because he sure as hell was not taking care of my requests. Needless to say, I never hooked up with these grunts again.

As a result of this one experience, I learned to recognize the sounds of rape from a great distance. This is a terrible thing to learn. Over a period of time, I would hear this sound again. One time I looked over at the captain to see if he understood what was happening. I never received any indication he knew or understood. And of course we never talked about anything.

This event occurred in 1968, and it still has an impact on my attempts to have intimate relationships with women. I have been single and alone most of my adult life. I will not make the first move when it comes to sex. I do not accept suggestive words, actions, or looks from a female as consent to have sex. If a female says she wants to have sex, I ask her to confirm this verbally several times. This kind of ruins the moment, don't you think?

I feel uncomfortable wrapping my arms around a female because this is a form of restraint and dominance. If a chick wants to leave me, I cannot argue or change her mind as this would impose my will on hers. I lost a wife this way.

I think about the teenager who was raped by the three armed men. I wonder how things have turned out in her life. I also consider what kind of people the rapists have become in their adult years. Did they make it home alive? Did God remove their legs before he sent them home? Would I want to sit with them today? Would they want to sit with me?

I have bought only one videocassette movie in my life. I own it and will keep it forever even though I don't own a device that plays cassettes. I have never watched the movie on this cassette, and I don't think I ever will. I saw the original movie in a theater.

Casualties of War, starring Michael J. Fox and Sean Penn, is about a squad of LRRPs that go on patrol and kidnap a Vietnamese female with the intent of abusing her. Michael J. Fox's character does not rape and turns the others in. The accused grunts in the movie do not spend a single day in jail.

In the early 1980s I joined a Vietnam veteran's therapy group headed by an ex-marine who had been blown up and then shot in an all-night battle. He carried the M60 machine gun, which the marines called a "hog." His buddies called him a "pig fucker" because he humped the hog. My email address for him to this day is "hog humper."

In the early 90s we held a going-away party for Dan, the ex-marine and veterans counselor, at an abandoned mine up in the hills. Everyone had at least two weapons, and there was no chance of running out of ammo. We had made pipe bombs out of PVC, cannon fuse, and black power. I brought out my stash of National Guard–acquired booby traps, flares, and simulated artillery rounds. We filled the ex-marine's cannon with so much black power that it tipped over backward when we touched it off to start our "mad minute" of continual group fire. We also had an endless supply of beer and whiskey.

Guests at the going-away party were all ex-military and included:

Budd, who was a brown water sailor on PBR (Patrol Boat River), which dropped off and picked up SEAL teams. He sometimes went along on their missions.

Dan had been a marine in Vietnam before He got blown up with a grenade and then shot during an all-night battle.

Jim had spent his tour as a LRRP (long-range recon patrol) for the First Infantry Division, the Big Red One.

Berry, who had done some spooky kind of things for rogue outfits in the central highlands, where the evil Phoenix Project had a base.

By about 0300 everyone in the group had passed out except for me, the ex-marine, and Berry. Berry told a story about coming up on two marines in Nam who had staked out and raped a Vietnamese girl. The jarheads were in the process of cutting her up with their Ka-Bar field knives. Berry killed the two marines and did a mercy killing on the critically injured female. The names of the two marines are on the memorial wall in Washington D.C. Berry carries so much guilt from this shooting that he is committing slow suicide with booze as we speak.

At first light the ex-marine and I drove off the hill and headed for town. As soon as we started rolling, I asked Dan if he had heard Berry's story. I said, "His story about killing the two marines is another piece of my personal trauma. I am not sure how it fits in, but at least it tells me there are other possibilities." I asked the ex-marine, Dan, who was a certified mental health professional and my long-time personal shrink, what he thought.

Dan said, "The message is, you and Berry both made the best possible decision you could with the information you had available at the time." Dan is a wise man.

After the going-away party, Dan moved to another small town in Oregon so he could continue working with veterans. About a year later I joined this group and would make the three-hundred-mile round trip each Tuesday evening. I never clicked with this group. I wanted to deal with things going on in my life as they related to Vietnam. They wanted to forget about Vietnam except to plan a return trip. I wanted no part of that.

One of the marines in this group had raped several times while in Vietnam. He told us once that he could not achieve climax unless he had a Ka-Bar knife at a female's throat. He was married for a while, which brings up some interesting questions. If he needed to rape to achieve climax, did his wife need to be raped for him to achieve climax? I don't know and don't want to know.

The result of all this is that I see a rape and turn it over to God. The movie sees a rape and turns the grunts in, but they don't do any time. Larry sees a rape and kills the two marines. The Ka-Bar marine rapes repeatedly and becomes addicted to the power. Jimmy jacks off behind a tree after a gunfight, and Grump creams his jeans while blowing up a wet fetus. My buddy jacked off to relieve tension in Vietnam, and the Afghanistan veteran gets jacked up during a mortar battle and jacks off afterward. The guilt I carried for thirty years because I humped the ground while on ambush seems tame after further consideration.

Childhood had taught me, and I had come to believe, that America was made up of the good guys. We were the kind of people who let the bad guys draw first before we blew them away. We stood in the middle of the street at high noon while the bad guys bushwhacked us from behind boulders.

I realize it is stupid to let the other guy shoot first in war. We ambush them and they ambush us; this is just the way things are. When we fight and die for the moral imperative, like in WWII, I love America. When we become obsessed with winning, without regard for what is right and just, is when I question our intent.

Every day in the field required a tremendous amount of effort just to stand up, let alone hump. The temperature on this day in the jungle of my mind was close to a million degrees in the shade. The only shade was under the brim of the five-pound steel helmet we wore on patrols. Gallons of salty sweat drenched my clothes and ran like a river down my back, rushing unimpeded into the crack of my ass and escaping along the crease that separates my ball sack from my legs. The front of my pants from the waist to my knees was discolored with the visible stain of my own sweat.

I breathed in pure liquid humidity and tried to separate the air from the moisture by spitting.

A person had to learn to love the jungles of Vietnam, because hate would leave you exhausted and defeated. The leeches that sucked my blood were every bit a part of God's plan the same way that the next step might or might not be followed by an explosion. The accidental discharge of an M79 grenade launcher could kill your buddy or make you laugh in embarrassment when it didn't travel the thirty-three feet or three rotations needed to arm the round. It's all part of the plan.

On one particular patrol, I was perhaps two squads back from the point element as we worked our way up a hill. The pace was agonizingly slow. We took three or four steps at a time and then bent over at the waist huffing and puffing while we shifted the weight of our rucksacks looking for the illusive position that promised to relieve the pain of the straps cutting into the flesh of our shoulders.

One of the grunts ahead of me in the column had given up. He dropped his rucksack and was balled up crying with his head in his hands and his hands on his knees. He couldn't go any farther and didn't care about anything including a court marshal, the gooks, the weather, or the sweat in the crack of my ass.

I tried to pump the dude up with jokes, but he had already told a sergeant to fuck off, so anything I said was a waste of time. I made a quick plan without anyone else's knowledge or consent and put it into effect. We were near the top of the hill, so I humped to the crest, dropped my rucksack, and returned to the broken troop.

The grunt gave me shit at first, but I wasn't having it. I strapped on his rucksack and took it to the top of the hill. He had no choice but to follow. Over the next hour, the rest of the company reached the crest and began to dig in. The CO was on the horn ordering supplies as I began constructing a fighting position.

The place we picked to RON (remain overnight) had been used by Americans before. We could see the scars of abandoned fox-holes and one particularly large spot that had been used as a trash dump. Apparently the Americans had spent an extended period of time at this location judging from the size of the trash pit.

The grunt that couldn't make it up the hill went into a dump site with his buddy. I was thinking that they were looking for easy digging, and if they found it they could die. We had been told to avoid dump sites and old foxholes because both sides liked to booby trap these places. The fact that I had carried the dude's rucksack meant as little to him as, you know, the sweat in the crack of my ass. He had turned lazy and lazy kills. Before I could yell at the grunts to get out of the dump site, they touched off a booby-trapped grenade. The lazy grunt died and his buddy was fucked up.

There was no reason to make the effort to get closer and have a look. The medic was already running there. I had learned early in my tour not to look at mangled bodies unless I had to. What is seen for a split second with the eyes remains in the mind forever. As far as easy digging goes, the rule is: if you find easy digging, you might as well go deep so your buddies will have a place to bury your dead body. Remember to always dig a new, fresh hole and be happy when you hit rocks or water—they don't explode.

Here is another typical war story. I don't remember where it took place, other than South Vietnam. I don't know what our mission was, other than climbing the hill in front of me. I don't know what month of the year it was, other than it was not monsoon season. I don't remember the real name of the grunt I was sharing point with, so I will call him Bubba.

It was critical to remember the important things, such as: which direction I was facing; not to put anything in my rucksack that I didn't need; always pack extra water, ammo, shoestrings, mosquito repellent, and radio batteries; and never to take the next step until you have surveyed every blade of grass for trip wires and those three short pieces of hard wire that poke out the top of a buried Bouncing Betty anti-personnel mine.

The point was made up of a black dude from the East Coast (Bubba) and me. We had walked out of level rice paddy ground and into semiheavy vegetation that covered a hill perhaps a thousand feet in elevation. It was hard work to break through the undergrowth while climbing. We traveled in single file to navigate terrain like this as it didn't make sense to break two trails up the same hill.

We had reached a point that was thirty meters short of a hogback ridge covered by short grass. As soon as we got to the grass, the walking would be easy—assuming Charlie was not waiting in ambush with a clear field of fire. Both Breeze and I were covered in sweat and breathing like a racehorse after the Kentucky Derby. We had outrun the rest of the company by twenty meters, so we took the opportunity to drop the rucksacks and catch our breath. I lit a smoke and jumped on top of a rock to look around. Bubba dropped to his ass without removing his rucksack and leaned back against a large boulder.

I heard someone farther down the hill yell, "Booby trap!" Within two seconds someone else a little closer gave the booby trap alarm. Others started sounding off with similar booby trap discoveries. We had walked into a minefield. This was not the first time we had walked into this problem, and it would not be the last. Bubba started looking over his rest site and quickly spotted more booby traps less than two feet from where he had plopped down. I gingerly un-assed the boulder and lowered myself to the ground. Upon looking around I spotted several of the improvised explosive devices in the area also.

The booby traps had been exposed through erosion. They appeared to be made of coke cans filled with explosives and shrapnel. The shrapnel could have been steel, glass, or rocks. I really didn't want to find out. It appeared the booby traps had been placed a long time before, and the erosion from the rain had washed off the covering soil. Once we saw the first booby trap and knew what to look for, I thought it was easy to spot more from a distance.

The company commander called Bubba and me back down the hill to talk things over. We retraced our steps while the commander got in touch with battalion to give them a SITREP (situation report). We huddled with the captain at the base of a large boulder. I argued that the mines were exposed and we should walk the whole company through the minefield. The captain didn't like my plan much, so he got back on the horn with battalion.

A few minutes later I heard the captain say, "Roger, out." The CO addressed our small huddled group and said, "The battalion commander is on his way to our location. He wants to take someone to the top of the ridge where the recon platoon was waiting with two engineers who have mine detectors. The engineers will use their detectors to clear a path for the rest of the company." There was silence followed by more silence as the captain looked from Bubba to me then back to Bubba. The captain broke the silence by saying, "Who wants to volunteer for this detail?"

After more tense seconds of additional silence, I jumped up and said, "I will do it, but if I die it will be your fault." Before anyone could reply, I walked off toward my rucksack. I have regretted that statement for more than forty years. It was a shitty thing to put a guilt trip on the captain like that. If I would have died, he may have carried that guilt the rest of his life. I did not want to be responsible for something like that, even if I was dead.

I retraced my steps back up the hill to my rucksack. If I was going to get a ride to the top of the hill, my rucksack was going with me. It would be dumb to hump my gear up a hill when I didn't have to. I strapped on my gear and began moving up the side of the hogback under the logic that the mines would be on the spine of the ridge and not the sides.

The battalion commanding officer and his XO (executive officer) showed up in their steel horse. The pilot was forced to hover four feet off the ground with the chopper's nose pointed toward the hillside. The pilot concentrated on not running his rotor blades into the ground. The colonel grabbed a handful of my rucksack to help pull me over the skids and into the belly of the chopper. The XO grabbed my M16 after I threw it on the floor and cleared it for me. I lay on the deck of the chopper until they dropped me off on top of the hill a few minutes later.

The engineers and I started down the hill with me in the lead. After a short distance, I turned on the engineers and yelled for them to spread the fuck out. "Don't get close to me," I said. "If I get blown up, I ain't taking anybody with me." My outburst got their attention and our spacing was adjusted accordingly. Fucking rookies, they didn't understand that a grunt's best friend is never closer than forty feet. Any closer and we became a danger to each other. Fucking mines.

We needed to travel about a half mile down the open hogback in a north-northwest direction to reach the company. The vegetation from the recon platoon's position to within a hundred feet of Charlie Company was nothing more than short grass. The engineers repeatedly suggested that they should be in the lead with their mine detectors. I had already developed a plan I liked better. About halfway down the hill, at a point where the hogback turned to the west, I called a halt to our small group and addressed the engineers like the buck sergeant I was.

I dropped my rucksack and said to the rookies, "You wait here while I go and find a booby trap. This way you will know what you are looking for. If I am correct, the booby traps are aluminum and I don't think your detectors can spot them." As I headed down the hill, one of the engineers asked how I was going to find a booby trap. Without looking back over my shoulder, I said, "I will either see a mine with my eyes, or you will see an explosion with yours. Either way, you will find out what the mines look like."

I continued down the hill with my M16 at the ready. I could see every blade of grass; if a fly had farted, I would have heard it. This is the crazy walk, near heat exhaustion, wired on adrenalin, lack of food and water, and full of fatigue. I was leaving behind mine detectors and relying on my eyes and instinct to do the job. This is the crazy walk of a man who is already dead. And if he is already dead, what difference does it make? How crazy can it be?

Within several feet of breaking out of the short grass and entering waist-high vegetation, I spotted one of the booby traps. I did a quick 360 scan of my immediate area to confirm that I had not overlooked other mines while coming down the hill. I signaled the two engineers standing some four hundred meters away to join me.

When the engineers arrived, I pointed out a booby trap beside the trail which ran the length of the hogback. They instantly knew what they were and began educating me about things I didn't care to know. When they finished their tutorial, I filled them in on the rest of my plan.

Charlie Company was hidden from our view by vegetation, but I knew they were less than thirty meters away down the hill. I told the engineers to clear a path from our location to the company.

One of the engineers asked where the company was. I hollered down the hill to make voice contact. The captain yelled back in response, and I told him the engineers needed to maintain voice contact so they could be guided to the company location.

The engineers understood that I had done my part by getting them there. It was time they took over. I assured them that I would cover their backs, as they would be busy. I walked back up the hill fifty meters to get out of blast range should the mission go badly. One hour later elements of the company started breaking into the open. That signaled a successful mission to me. One of the best parts of the day was that my rucksack was already halfway up the hill.

In the late afternoon, the company commander notified everyone that he had requested a new supply of M16 ammo. He told us to fire off all our old ammo, clean our weapons, and acquire a new standard issue. Apparently original M16s with the split muzzle flash suppressor like the weapons we carried jammed on a regular basis and the brass were blaming it on dirty ammo and weapons. Allowing us to fire off all our ammo was like taking kids to the county fair. The seriousness of this weapons failure never really registered with me until I saw the five M16s left behind by the NVA after they overran our recon platoon.

Many times we had no problem getting our weapons to fire. On one particular day we were occupying a hill somewhere in Vietnam. I can remember very little about the hill's location or height. I don't have a clue as to our mission or the time of year. We had developed the hill's defensive posture through the use of sandbags, bunkers, foxholes, and perimeter wire complete with trip flares and claymores.

One of the bunkers occupied by Charlie Company on the northeast corner of the hill contacted Charlie six and asked permission to test-fire its M60. Charlie six informed the position that we were in a restricted contact zone during daylight hours. Charlie six went on to inform the requesting body that a mandatory curfew would go into effect at 1800 hours.

At 1800 hours the contact status of all the surrounding area would transition into a free-fire zone. Anything or anyone in the free-fire zone was determined to be the enemy. One minute a farmer in his field would be a local going about his business, and the next minute that same local would be declared the enemy and you could legally kill them. This is not to imply that being legal was a prerequisite to many of the things we did. The M60 crew would be allowed to test-fire its weapons after the 1800-hour transition.

Where had I heard this line of crap before? It sounded like a grade school trick. The voices of the M60 crew told me there was something else going on. For one, we had been in this fighting position for more than a few days. The M60 crew knew the rules as well as everyone else. I decided to go over to their position and check things out. When I got there, I found two grunts that had set up their M60 in a foxhole next to a well-built sandbagged bunker. As I looked to the west from their position approximately four hundred meters, I could see a water buffalo grazing in the rice paddies. To the right of the water buffalo I saw a military-age male (MAM) working on the raised dike between two rice paddies with a hand tool similar to a hoe. Farther to the right I saw a military-age female (MAF) using a reed basket to haul dirt from the MAM to another spot along the dike. It appeared they were repairing a busted portion of the dike.

The two grunts with the M60 were counting down the minutes to 1800 hours. They were telling each other that the fucking gooks would probably go out after dark and plant booby traps designed to kill Americans. They ranted that the fucking bitch was probably

VC (Vietnamese Communist) who gave blow jobs to Charlie for a bowl of rice. I could see where this was going. They were building verbal justification for something they had already planned to do. I decided to hang around and watch them test-fire. I wondered if the gooks knew about the curfew. Shortly before the magic 1800 hours arrived, I noticed a change in the movement pattern of the two gooks. The MAF had left her reed basket at the spot where she had dumped the dirt. The MAM had collected his tools and was walking down the dike toward the female as she walked up the dike toward him. When they met he handed her the tools and turned around to collect his water buffalo.

The two grunts were heating up the airwaves seeking permission to test-fire their weapons. The male gook had collected his water buffalo and was driving it out of the rice fields. The female gook was about thirty yards from exiting the rice paddy with the hand tools.

They received permission to test-fire the M60. They didn't waste any time. They walked M60 rounds up to the female and knocked her off the dike. They then engaged the male. I saw 7.62 rounds walking through the rice paddy toward the male, and then he disappeared; he possibly went to ground or maybe he got hit and knocked off the dike. They engaged the water buffalo next. The water buffalo took several hits, but it is a tough animal to bring down. A voice on the radio repeated, "Cease-fire, cease-fire, cease-fire." The curfew was in place, but a cease-fire had been achieved by order. The grunts began critiquing their shooting. As I walked away, an officer or possibly an NCO went over and had a chat with the boys.

I had always believed that murder was a violent act committed by people who were angry or terribly upset or possessed by evil or some other highly emotional state of mind. These two grunts were calm and laughing. They had decided to kill devoid of emotion. They did it because they could. To them it was like, "What's the big deal, man? It doesn't mean anything." I think I was raised on a different planet.

Patches

Some nights I would lie on the ground after a long day's march, calm and at ease during my watch with the radio microphone held close to my ear and my M16 in reach. Sometimes I was reminded about how I got here. The final word is that I felt fortunate to be able to hump with the young men and leaders who were not much older than we were.

At an early age while working on a ranch and sleeping alone in a bunk house, I had dreams that became plans to sail across the ocean on a ship, fly around the world in a plane, join the military, make sergeant E-5, and not get an article 15 court-martial. I also planned to go to war. I didn't care who it was with or where it was at. I was innocent, thinking war was a man's game where the good guys beat the bad guys because God was on our side. I discovered in the jungle that God does not choose sides or declare winners; only mankind does that.

These childhood dreams would all play out with unexpected twists including the part about not getting a full-time permanent job before I turned forty years old. I watched my dad work his whole life just to support the eight of us in a small company-owned house. It seemed like such a waste; very little of his life was his own. I vowed to live first in honor of his labor and then get work from age forty to sixty-five before retiring. Somehow this plan worked out, and I was offered a full-time job with the forest service within two months of turning forty. I had gotten most everything I had dreamed of as a kid. Not only did I get everything, but in some cases I received much more than I knew was available. The perfect childhood brought me here; I hold few regrets. If one thing were to change, then all things would need to change and I had no need for that. I feel that regret is the pity potty.

As a personal guideline for the writing of this book, I have chosen not to develop in depth the characters that represent my biological and extended families and friends. I speak *about* them but not *for* them, if possible. There is a line where I begin to feel that I am violating their privacy, and that makes me very uncomfortable. I may say or not say something that could hurt feelings without intent. That is not the purpose of this account. It is best if I tell my own stories as the most experienced critic of myself available. My family members have their own options.

At the beginning we were a large family from a small logging town named Seneca, in rural Eastern Oregon. My three older brothers were followed by a sister before I was born, and my younger sister was the last in line before my parents called it quits. Being the fifth of six children, I presented few new or unexpected challenges to my parents, who often reminded us that they have in the past and can still to this day, even after they are dead, see and hear everything, all the time, forever and at any distance.

No matter what I did, it wasn't as bad as the first sibling who did it. I had a built-in behavioral cousin to protect and guide me through childhood. My four older siblings opened all the doors I would need to go through to reach adulthood. They sometimes beat me up but just as often protected me from others.

In the company town of Seneca, we had three sets of bunk beds along the walls in a small room in the back of our house. Six kids sharing the same bedroom was a real hoot. If you have lots of big brothers and sisters, you know what I mean. The crazy stories and embarrassed recollections we siblings share from that period still reverberate around bouts of unanimous laughter. I have no anxiety, fears, or trauma from my early childhood years, but later I would have plenty of time to collect my fair share of those things.

By the time I turned eleven, it was clear to my parents and anyone else who was paying attention that I was a cross between the Tasmanian devil and Speedy Gonzales. I was the shortest kid in my class and the class above and below me. They called me a cutup and a class clown. I was fearless of others bigger, faster, or stronger, although few were faster and stronger. I felt invulnerable, destined to outdraw Matt Dillon at the beginning of the *Gunsmoke*, TV show and to outflank the enemy and win the day on the *Combat*, TV series. I would defend the honor of a female on the *Have Gun—Will Travel*, show and sing to the rodeo crowd on the Saturday *Sky King* Hour. My head was filled with visions of defending the weak and upholding justice faster than a speeding bullet. My parents were convinced that my head was filled with different ways to injure or kill myself.

As a young child, I would see a picture of a paratrooper and the next day would find enough string to tie a sheet to myself so I could jump off the corner of the house. I discovered that sheets do not inflate at ten feet off the ground. I needed to find a taller building that didn't have parents around. It's hard to believe, but my best friend, Don Leslie, "Tuffy," tested my paratrooper idea off the top of the Wrights house. The Wrights had two good-looking daughters, and Tuffy would do anything to impress a girl. Tuffy didn't get hurt on this day, but it wasn't because we didn't try. We abandoned the idea of hooking the sheet to ourselves and started fixing a handkerchief to a small rock, which sometimes worked well.

School broke for summer vacation in June. On the last day of school, we were told to come in at 1:00 p.m. to pick up our report cards. Tuffy and I took this opportunity to go down to the local creek where I would try to drown myself. As luck would have it, Tuffy recognized the meaning of my head sinking under water for a second time in a row and the "blurb-blurb" sound of a drowning friend in time to pull me to the safety of the riverbank.

We made it back to school just in time to collect our report cards. My mother was waiting in the classroom with Mrs. Hendrix. This was not good. My mother commented that I was soaking wet, but she didn't chew me out. I was about to be slapped around in a different way. My report card said I would be held back in the fifth grade for another year. Mrs. Hendrix told me it was because I had not learned my states and capitals. She asked me if I remembered the rule. I confirmed that she had repeated several times over the year that a failure to memorize the states and capitals would result in that person repeating the fifth grade.

There may have been other reasons to hold me back, but I will never know. I learned that in Texas it was common to hold large boys back a year or two in grade school. The result was that Texas produced some of the biggest, strongest high school football teams in the nation. All of Texas loves its Friday night football games. Across the nation in the 1950s it was not uncommon for teachers to hold small-statured boys back a year so they might possibly grow and be similar in size to their classmates.

On the other hand, I had not learned my states and capitals. The cards had been dealt; I would no longer be in the same class as all those I had grown up with. The upside of this was that I would be in the same class as Linda, my girlfriend, and that reality pretty much neutralized all the bad things. They don't put a stamp on your forehead when you fail a grade, so it is not like everyone in the world would know unless I told them or had it printed in a book.

My mom and I left the school together and walked across the street to our house, where she dropped another bombshell. She said that after we got home we would pack some clothes in a bag because Jim and Jean Sproul had offered me a summer job. Mom said that bright and early the next morning Jean Sproul would take me out to their ranch in the northwest corner of Bear Valley. I thought this was great. I was eleven years old and had a job. There were eighth graders in town that did not have a summer job. I quickly forgot about failing the fifth grade.

Mrs. Sproul failed to show at first light. I drove everyone crazy waiting for her car to pull up in front of our house. She arrived about 1:00 p.m., we said good-bye and this and that, and we finally hit the road. Jean Sproul was a beautiful lady and, even though I would work on the Bear Valley ranch for the next two summers, I do not believe my eyes ever saw any part of her body below the breasts. To this day I could not confirm that she had legs, but I know for a fact she had breasts and beautiful long blonde hair. I'm not really sure about the long blonde hair. I am sure about the breasts. Boys of eleven are not that far removed from their mother's tits, and they begin looking for a replacement the morning after they are weaned.

When we arrived at the ranch, I was told to get settled in the bunkhouse. As I came out of my new home, I met Jim Sproul for the first time. Jim was one of the biggest men I had ever seen. He weighed more than three hundred pounds. He could lift up an ox, carry it to the dinner table, and after eating it go play giggle with his wife. He could go bear hunting with a toothpick and the bear would be at a disadvantage.

Jim was one of my first real-life heroes. He could drive a Cat, blow things up with dynamite, build a lake, ride a horse all day, fix a fence, cut and stack hay, weld steel, and pull his .22 pistol out of a holster while moving on horseback to fire one round and kill a rattlesnake. I could throw a bottle or bottle cap into the air and he could shoot it, first time, every time. Jim was a big man, this was a big ranch, and Jean had big breasts.

Jim walked me around the barnyard to show me what to feed, how much to feed, and who to feed it to. He told me I was to get myself up in the morning, do the chores, put the separator together, and stage the milk to run through it when the cooks began work.

All the information about the chores was being stored in my mind as we made the rounds. Jim then took me to a fence that overlooked the lower pasture where the milk cows, geese, and a few horses grazed leisurely. He pointed out a white pony with large black spots that he called Patches. Jim said the horse would be mine for the rest of the summer, and the first thing the next day we would put a saddle on him and see how I got along with that Welsh pony.

I couldn't have been farther away from failing the fifth grade if they had sent me to the moon. If this was punishment, then I couldn't imagine what success would be like. My last thoughts before going to bed that night were, "Jean has big breasts."

The next day we moved Patches and some other horses out of the lower pasture and into a collecting corral. Jim got a rope on Patches and moved him into the barnyard where he was hitched at a staging area. Jim then picked out a saddle that looked like it might fit me and rounded up a halter and blanket made for a small horse. We put the gear on Patches and let him stand at the hitching post for about two hours because he had not been saddled since the fall before and his disposition would be a little surly. I would find out over the next two years that Patches was a little surly most of the time and a lot surly some of the time. He had a right to be cantankerous because in human years Patches was older than I was.

After lunch Big Jim fixed me up with a straw hat and a pair of spurs. He told me to mount the pony and hang on, because that surly critter would sure as hell try and cause me to have a wreck. I took the reins off the hitching post and pointed Patches toward an open space in the barnyard. I didn't want him bucking me into a rail fence. I grabbed some short reins, latched onto the saddle horn with my left hand and planned to put my foot into the stirrup and be in the saddle before Patches knew what hit him. That was my plan anyway.

As soon as my weight hit the left stirrup and before my right leg could swing over his butt and into the other stirrup, Patches was off running and bucking. He bounced me up and out of the saddle, so I tucked my thighs under the bucking rolls while I re-acquired the reins. This all worked out really well. Big Jim and his two sons hollered and hooted and waved their arms to help Patches buck a little harder. I threw my right arm up in the air just like the real cowboys on TV. Patches slowed down to a walk, and I spurred him one more time. Patches was a smart horse. Before our relationship was over, he would leave me sitting on the ground wondering what had happened more times than I could count. He would dump me when he was ready, not when I was.

Patches would become my main horse for the next two years. Big Jim, the other ranch hands, and I would go down into the Murderers Creek country each summer and round up cattle for three or four days in a row. Once we had collected two hundred head of cows and bulls, we would herd them on a two-day drive back to the main ranch.

Big Jim would go through two or three horses a day, while I rode patches every day, all day. Jim's horses were so big that I had to book a flight just to reach the stirrups. He could exhaust one horse in the morning and another one in the afternoon. If we rode late, he would carry a third horse to the dinner table and eat him, hooves, horseshoes, saddle horn, and all. What could be better?

When we started the two-day drive to the main ranch, I would saddle Patches at 4:00 a.m. We would open the gate at 4:30 a.m., and the lead cow would start trotting up the road. Big Jim would give me a shot of whiskey to help cut the morning chill and we would hoot and holler the cows until our voices gave out. I was eleven years old and had stories grown men couldn't tell.

As time went on, Patches and I learned to do some tricks together. Every time we would approach a barbwire fence, I would gallop Patches ahead of the pack and dismount to open and hold the gate for everyone else. After they passed through, I would go into slow motion shutting the gate so all those cowboys could get way ahead of us.

Horses don't like to be the last in line; it's not in their nature. They like to run with the herd and maybe even lead the group. So if you hold a horse back, they get real antsy and want to run hard to catch up. This is just what I wanted.

After latching the gate, I would hold a tight rein on Patches and turn him to face the other riding stock out in front of us. Patches would paw his right front hoof on the ground and blow his nose; his body would quiver just a little and his head would shake. I would grab the saddle horn with both my hands and holler, "Giddy up!" I brought my feet off the ground and tucked both knees into my chest. I would hang off the left side of Patches as he reached full gallop in two strides. I would bring my feet down, tap the ground, and swing up into the saddle just like Roy Rogers in the Saturday morning TV show. God, we were good.

My routine was great that summer. I would do the chores as soon as I got up in the morning. My next job was to corral, catch, and saddle Patches so I could ride over to the high forty and bring the other horses into the barnyard. Lots of times I would have to wait before anyone else would be up to fix breakfast.

The meals in this place were fit for a king. Big tables, big stacks of food, Big Jim, big ideas, and big breasts floated around free like oil on water.

After breakfast I might be told to take Patches and mend a line of barbwire fence. Other times we would load several horses in a trailer, drive for an hour, and spend all day moving cattle. I might hook up with the ranch hand to move bulls or steers and, if I was lucky, other horses. Horses were fun to move because they ran most of the time. Steers would trot, but they didn't run like horses. The cows were slow and dumb, but the bulls were temperamental and scary dangerous.

Patches knew how to move livestock better than I did. He also knew how to dump me in a pile whenever he got tired of my kicking his ribs with my boot heels. As an inexperienced kid, I was all "gallop and go." Patches was more like "hold up and whoa."

Sometimes I would see a calf cut from the group and head for the hills, so I would put some leather on Patches' flank and giddy up after that critter. I wanted to follow that calf's every move. My eyes, my senses, everything would be focused on that calf. Patches had other plans. He often would trot under a tree that had branches sticking out just above the height of the saddle horn. I would have a terrible wreck, and when the dust settled Patches would be standing six feet away eating grass while I was picking pine needles out of my focus.

On another occasion I had Patches in a full gallop on the tail of a fast calf. We were running and jumping sagebrush, dodging and jumping sagebrush, running and I assumed jumping—but Patches dodged left and I went straight ahead. When the dust cleared, Patches was standing six feet away eating grass while I was trying to separate the sagebrush from my assumptions.

At one point I had learned not to hang on to the saddle horn when Patches jumped a log. Up to that time whenever we jumped a log, I would end up in front of the saddle horn balanced on his neck because the stiff arm holding the saddle horn acted like a loaded spring; as soon as Patches kicked off with his rear legs that spring would throw me up on his neck. Armed with this new wisdom, I would go out of my way to find a log for Patches to jump. One day we were at a full gallop when up comes a big log. I stood up in the stirrups and leaned forward over the saddle horn waiting for Patches to raise his front legs then kick with his hind legs and sail over the log. Patches decided to stop. I ended up wrecked on the other side of the log nursing my new wisdom. Patches was standing six feet away eating grass.

The worst wreck I ever had while riding Patches damn near took my head off. We had been branding calves all day long. The neighbors and drop-by friends had worked hard, eaten a good meal, and settled their whims with a couple shots of whiskey. Around 4:00 p.m. everyone loaded up stock and headed home. My last job before starting evening chores was to run the roping horses up to the high forty pasture. The horses knew where to go as well as I did. Patches had to trot to keep up. The herd milled around the gate while I dismounted to open it for them. As soon as I got out of their way, the roping horses entered their forty-acre playground. With that job complete, Patches and I turned south and headed home.

Patches didn't wear shoes, so I got him off to the left side of the road so we could gallop in the grass. About two hundred yards from the ranch stood a large telephone pole that had a three-quarter-inch steel cable guy wire tied to the pole on one end and staked to the ground on the other. Patches and I had taken this path dozens of times, so I didn't pay much attention as we approached the guy wire. Patches had a long day also and maybe by accident or out of plain meanness he was a little to the left of our usual path. At the last second, I realized the guy wire was going to hit me. Pure instinct raised both my arms straight up in the air just in time for the guy wire to catch me under the armpits. I was thrown backward off the pony and landed square on my back knocking every particle of air out of my lungs—and I think knocking me out also. When I regained my senses, Patches was standing six feet away eating grass, I had terrible marks under my armpits, and I held a set of broken reins.

I will always remember Patches as a sturdy, reliable horse with a mind and manner of his own. As befitting the legacy of an old Welsh pony, I will end this story with a parade.

At the annual 62 Days Celebration, Patches and I were transformed into a young Indian boy and his pony. Jean Sproul mixed baby oil and cocoa to darken my body. She trimmed a horse's mane to make a wig for my head. I rode bareback that day and used my knees and a hair rope to control the pony. Patches was sometimes that gentle.

Of course, enough was never enough for me. Even though we won the show with our looks, I tried to show off more by having Patches walk sideways, first to the left and then again to the right. I did this several times until Patches got fed up with my games and put an end to it by raring up on his hind legs and scaring the hell out of me. The crowd clapped and yelled approval while I wore a nervous smile and pretended like it was all part of the plan.

As luck would have it, my mom and sisters were standing in a perfect spot to see this beautiful pony rare up on its hind legs with me on his back. I hadn't intended for things to go like this, but as usual Patches would have his way.

He was a fine pony. I can still see him to this day, standing six feet away eating grass while I sit in a cloud of dirt chewing on my pride.

It is possible that I had the best childhood in the world. My war games playground was large and close. I had money in my pocket and a girlfriend on my arm. My same-age friends had hung up their cowboy gear and started to develop an eye for young perky breasts they had discovered blooming in their classes.

I started wearing a white US Navy work cover my oldest brother had sent me from his ship in Japan. I used a stick or a rubber band gun as an army rifle and spent my spare time digging foxholes in an empty sagebrush field across the state highway. I would crawl through the mine-infested, sagebrush-covered field using every dirt clod as if it were a hand grenade. We played a war game high-lighted by the words, "I shot you first." Someone always won the war.

The war games would not last long because high school sports loomed close ahead. I dreamed of winning medals on the football field. I was 125 pounds and five three. My mother had dreams of me being crushed to death, so she needed constant reassurances about the sport's safety.

At the end of football season my senior year, I was selected as a first-team all-conference middle linebacker. Basketball practice started in December, and on the day team pictures were sched-uled, I encountered a bump in my path to manhood.

I waved good-bye to my mother while thanking her for wash-ing my basketball uniform. I opened the door of the '47 Ford I had bought for fifty dollars with money I earned thinning trees with a chain saw the summer before.

"If I didn't wash your uniform I don't know who would?" my mother said.

"Sorry, Mom," I said with an understanding smile. "I will give you more warning next time, but they just told us about the pictures this morning. I have to go; the varsity basketball team photos are happening in less than ten minutes. Bye. Love you."

As I backed out of the driveway, I was careful not to scrape the white picket fence. I drove north on Egan Street and then took a left on West Tyler Street. It is five blocks from Egan Street to Highway 395 and then less than a hundred yards to the high school. I had traveled the first four blocks and started to slow down for the approaching intersection when suddenly the front of my car exploded. My windshield was shattered but still intact.

What the hell happened? My car glided to a stop. I tried to open the driver's door, but it was jammed. What the hell happened? I slammed into the door as hard as I could with my left shoulder. The door began to move with a metal-on-metal scraping sound. I hit the door again, and it opened enough to allow me to exit. My windshield was broken with a thousand lines going off in as many different directions. What the hell happened? I turned around to see a Honda motorbike lying twisted and broken on the road to my east. I walked four steps toward the rear of my car and saw the legs of a person on the pavement. I took two more steps and heard a girl screaming. I saw her boyfriend, the senior class president and honor student, lying on the ground. Randy lay there forever. The ambulance would take him to the hospital, and Randy would die a week later. His family would grieve, and the ramifications for the other lives involved in the accident would begin to mature.

My mother told me many years later as she was dying of cancer how she crossed the street for more than twenty years to avoid coming face to face with Randy's mother. On one occasion, Mrs. Russell followed my mother and cornered her in an aisle of a store. She begged my mother to quit avoiding her and said that she held no blame for anyone in our family concerning her son's death. My mother and I cried together.

The question that crossed my mind was, "Why him and not me?" He was the class president, and I was a jock and the class clown. I would graduate from high school and go to war in search of answers to some of life's mysteries. I would come to know death in the war, but I would struggle to have a relationship with life.

Within the course of two months during my senior year, I will experience a traumatic death and an attempted gay reach around, also referred to as a "Mormon" or "jailhouse handshake," from a basketball teammate while on an overnight trip to Klamath Falls, Oregon. I had no clue what was happening at the time, but I would figure it out after joining the army, because they talk about homosexuals and death a lot.

Volunteering for the military seemed like the natural thing to do after high school. Both my father and mother had worked in the Portland shipyards during WWII. All three of my oldest brothers had enlisted and done a hitch in either the navy or the army.

I signed papers to join the army for three years so I could go airborne before older kids told me I should have signed up for two years because the army would beg me to jump out of a plane once I had enlisted. In an effort to correct my mistake, I volunteered for the draft, but the lady at the Grant County courthouse said she already had enough draftees to meet her monthly quota. I told her about the mistake I had made signing up for three years, and she did her thing and drafted me just before I was to be called up for an extended period three. I feel that if I had been required to do a year in the army after returning from Vietnam, then I would still be in the stockade for either substance abuse or participation in the asshole elimination program.

The induction center in Boise, Idaho, welcomed me and two other high school classmates. After receiving a physical, we put our clothes back on and stood in formation to take an oath vowing to protect the nation from all enemies both foreign and domestic. My best friend from high school and I were in the same row of recruits. When we came to attention, he locked his knees and stood tall with his right hand raised. Two minutes later he was flat on his back having passed out from cutting off the circulation when he locked his knees.

Our first two weeks of basic training was everything the army was not supposed to be. We could not be issued sheets or uniforms or boots because they didn't have these necessary items in stock. If you have ever been to Fort Lewis, Washington, in January, you know it is not a place to go marching around in civilian clothes. It was cold, wet, and miserable with no way to dry out our clothes. My shoes and socks were soggy, but I put them on and marched around in the cold rain singing songs about dying in a combat zone and Jody banging my old lady.

My overall impression was that they didn't push us hard enough physically in training. I thought we should run farther and more often. I was disappointed at their standards and let the drill instructors know about it. The drill instructors let me know that the army was not a democracy and that they couldn't care less about what I thought.

"Drop to the ground and give me twenty push-ups, you maggot piece of shit," the instructor said as he put his face nose to nose with the violator of whatever rule he chose to reinforce. Drill instructors have made an art of the ability to have bad breath every day, all day. When they positioned their nose at the nose of a recruit, yelling at the top of their lungs and spewing spittle wrapped in horrific breath, we took notice.

"Drop and give me twenty," the instructor would yell. I would drop and give him forty. After a couple of times doubling the push-up request, they tended to leave me alone.

It takes a special person to be a garrison soldier. I am not a special person, and my legs are short. I could run the obstacle course in minimum time, fire expert on the range, and achieve the maximum score on the fitness test, but I was no good at marching and parade drill. I was so bad, in fact, that a major told the drill instructors not to let me march in our graduation ceremony because I would screw it up.

The major was right. I was assigned to be the fire watch for our barracks during the graduation. When the platoon returned from the ceremonies, they found me passed out on my bunk after having consumed the better part of a pint of whisky. Apparently I was no better at drinking than I was at marching. The drill instructor had me pegged, though; he made the offhand comment that I would probably make a damn good combat soldier even though I sucked at drill and ceremony. He may have noticed how I could rally the platoon to win the shooting and physical training trophies given for the best platoon performance at the end of each training cycle. Some other platoon won the drill and ceremony award, no doubt a reflection of my marching skills.

Advanced individual training (AIT) is the second stage of the military's effort to mold young men into killers that would eat burnt dead babies. It was also the place where recruits learned their military occupational specialties (MOS). It is difficult to question the method by which the army selects an individual's MOS.

The army is the oldest continuous bureaucracy in the United States. Many large corporations model their internal structure after the military. The military, backed by hundreds of years of experience, has determined that a unit commander does best when he has between three and six elements under his command. A lieutenant commands four squads, a captain may command four platoons, a colonel commands four companies, and a general commands four battalions. Four is the standard number of units, but the true number will vary between three and six depending on the circumstances. The military knows something about leadership, and corporations have taken notice.

The army decided in its great wisdom that I would do well on a mortar team. Mortars come in different sizes, but the concept remains consistent: You start by placing a metal base plate on the ground and then attach a three- or four-foot-long tube onto the base plate. A projectile is then dropped down the tube igniting a prepared charge that will launch the projectile toward a target. The mortar is a perimeter defense weapon and is described as "high-angle indirect fire support." The MOS designation for a mortar man is 11C. It is as close as you can get to being an infantryman, who has an MOS of 11B.

For the first time in my life, I paid attention in class. A great deal of certainty indicated that my next stop would be Vietnam, and the skills I learned in AIT (advanced individual training) would come in handy. Maybe I did too well during AIT. They may have seen that I was capable of handling multiple weapons systems based on test scores or field performance with the mortars. No matter the reasoning behind it, my next set of orders was for Fort Hood, Texas, home of the "Hell on Wheels," Second Armored Division. My MOS was changed from infantry to tanks. I had a problem with this decision, and it would take me three months and a brush with an article 15 to correct the error.

The thing I liked most about Texas was when I crossed the border to leave the state. Don't get me wrong. I liked the armadillos and the possums. I loved the horizon-to-horizon scenery and that one tree between Fort Hood and Austin, which remains a constant joy and a reminder that some places had trees that covered whole hillsides and sometimes even entire mountain ranges.

On my first day in Fort Hood, I reunited with my best friend from grade school, Don Leslie. I knew that Don was stationed in Fort Hood with twenty thousand other troops, but I didn't know how I would find him. Having just arrived on the base, I stood in line to collect my travel pay when I saw a detail of five troops marching by. I recognized Don in the group and called out his name. We hooked up and exchanged addresses so we could spend all our off-duty time together.

Don was receiving skin grafts at a world-class burn center on the Fort Hood reservation. Tuffy, as he was called, had spent a year with the First Cavalry Division in Vietnam. He had severe burns on his chest and face that required constant professional medical attention and some occasional weed to self-medicate his PTSD (post-traumatic stress disorder). Tuffy and I would spend our weekends together getting drunk and looking for fights in Texas bars. I was more successful at finding altercations than Tuffy was.

Three times a week my unit would put sheathed bayonets on the ends of our rifles and train for riot control. We were practicing the techniques we would use to put a bayonet in the face of an American citizen to deny them the First Amendment rights that came with citizenship. After I developed an understanding of what we were doing, I would consistently volunteer to play the role of a protester for this training. The selected group of role players dressed in civilian clothes would taunt and harass the assembled lines of bayonets.

The unit I was in also conducted three full inspections a week. That might be fine for some people, but I was a terrible garrison soldier with a desire to be anywhere that didn't have me putting a bayonet in a teenage American's face. I couldn't think of a thing that I needed from this place called Texas, except Tuffy; he still had lessons to teach me as he had already been to Vietnam for one tour.

Tuffy showed me how to score weed in a matchbox from a dude in another barrack. After the first couple of hits off of Don's pipe, I no longer needed to go airborne; when the paratroopers stepped out of a plane, they simply floated to the ground. After smoking the pipe, I could step out of a plane and walk on clouds.

Every month the army would pay me eighty-two dollars for my efforts. I would spend the money on booze, weed, and more booze. It didn't take long for the three-inspections-a week outfit I was in to take notice that I was not paying to have my laundry done. During one inspection the captain got nose to nose with me and reamed my ass for being such a disappointment to this man's army. I stood at attention with a big smile on my face. You do not stand at attention with a big smile on your face in the military. The captain told me to wipe that shit-eating grin off my face and asked me what my fucking problem was.

"Sir, I said, "The men in Vietnam are fighting a real war while we act like a bunch of toy soldiers without their mommas. This is a game, sir, and I need to go to Vietnam where everyone plays for real."

The next day the company commander sat down with me in his office. I repeated my desire to go to Vietnam, and the captain allowed me to submit a request for transfer, Military Form 1049. While filling out the request, I changed my MOS back to11C, even though the army wanted me to be a tanker. I could have been in a sixty-ton steel coffin in Vietnam, but my boots belonged on the ground the same way I needed to pack my home on my back and live by a foxhole about the same size as a grave.

I received new orders for Hawaii a month later, and my MOS was listed as 11C. I was back in the infantry and headed for a tropical island. The thirty-day leave I took between Texas and Hawaii gave me the time to break up with my girlfriend and make my last wishes known in a sealed letter to one of my brothers. My childhood fantasies were becoming real. The reality may have been different than I had dreamed, but the outcome was no less to my liking.

The tropical heat of Hawaii slapped me in the face with its heavy humidity as I got off the plane. I had to learn to breathe a different way so the humidity did not end up in my lungs and drown me as I crossed the tarmac.

A military bus took me to the legendary Schofield Barracks on the island of Oahu. The driver directed me to the headquarters of the Fourth Battalion and told me to report with my orders so they could assign me a barrack. The clerk behind the desk noted the 11C MOS on my orders and assigned me to Echo, the heavy weapons company of the 4/3 infantry regiment. The Old Guard's Fourth Battalion had been practicing jungle warfare techniques in the steep, vegetation-covered mountains of Hawaii for more than two years.

The Fourth Battalion of the Third Infantry Regiment, the Old Guard, would join the 3/1, Always First, the 1/20 Sykes Regulars, and sometimes the 4/21 Gimlets to form the Eleventh Light Infantry Brigade's Jungle Warriors. The Eleventh LIB would join up with the 198th and the 196th Light Infantry Brigades to form the basis of the American Division, which would relieve Task Force Oregon.

In February 1967 Gen. Westmoreland authorized the creation of Task Force Oregon and charged it with the operational responsibility for the three southernmost provinces of the I Corps, Vietnam. This allowed the marines to concentrate its forces in the Con Thien and Khe Sanh areas, which were in the process of being besieged by the North Vietnamese Army.

Task Force Oregon was made up of the 196th Light Infantry Brigade, the first brigade of the 101st Airborne Division and the third brigade of the Twenty-fifth Infantry Division, later redesignated the Third Brigade, Fourth Infantry Division. Task Force Oregon became operational on April 20, 1967, when troops from the 196th LIB landed at the Chu Lai Airstrip and immediately began search operations around the base camp. Soldiers from the Third Brigade, Fourth Division started conducting search and destroy operations in southern Quang Ngai province, and in May, the First Brigade, 101st airborne paratroopers arrived at Duc Pho for operations in the jungles west of there.

Early operations conducted by Task Force Oregon included Malheur 1 and Malheur 11, Hood River, Benton, and Cook. On September 11, 1967, Operation Wheeler was launched against elements of the Second North Vietnamese Division working in the area northwest of Chu Lai.

On September 22, 1967, Brig. Gen. Samuel W. Koster assumed command of the task force, replacing Maj. Gen. Richard T. Knowles, and three days later Task Force Oregon became the American Division, composed of the 196th, 198th, and Eleventh Light Infantry Brigades, even though the latter two organizations were still training in the United States.

The American Division has a unique history that began in WWII. They relieved the marines who were fighting in the Pacific theatre on islands including Guadalcanal, Leyte, Bougainville, and the Solomon's. The so-called mop-up operations the American was charged with would last for more than three months on Guadalcanal and result in many Southern Cross casualties.

The American Division is the only US Army division ever formed outside the continental United States. The division also has the distinction of being the only US Army division with a name designation as opposed to a numbered identification such as the First Infantry, Second Infantry, and so on. The unit would later receive a numerical designation as the Twenty-third Infantry Division, but it is generally referred to as the American Division.

The complete history of the American Division can be found on the American Division Veterans Association website at www.americal.org. Different aspects of the American history can also be found at www.buffgrunt.com under history/roots. More information can be found in the US Army Center of Military History as well as Wikipedia.

Many men have served "Under the Southern Cross" with pride, courage, and professionalism, meeting the enemy in each encounter from Guadalcanal to the occupation of Japan during WWII. The true stories of the division's achievements are carried by the names on the tombstones at Arlington National Cemetery and the whispered memories of its aging veterans who must always remember.

The American was constituted May 24, 1942, and consisted of the 164th Infantry Regiment, the 132nd Infantry Regiment, and the 182nd Infantry Regiment plus support and artillery. The division adopted the motto "Under the Southern Cross" in reference to the constellation in the Southern Hemisphere known as, "Crux."

Units of the American Division saw their first full-scale battle with the enemy on October 26, 1942, when waves of enemy soldiers assaulted the positions of the Second and Third Battalions, 164th

Infantry, in an attempt to break through to Henderson Field. After two days of fierce fighting in the Battle of Henderson Field, more than a thousand enemy dead were found in front of the positions of the Americal Division.

The Americal Division in WWII was spawned from Task Force 6814 in New Caledonia where the American troops debarked. The mission of Task Force 6814 was to hold New Caledonia against enemy attack. The Americal Division's name was derived from combining the defense of New Caledonia and the American mission. The phrase "Americans in New Caledonia" became "Americal."

The other regiments of the Americal would be drawn into Guadalcanal and not announce a defeat of the enemy there until February 9, 1943. The Americal would take a break to train and refit while in a semidefensive posture.

In March 1943 the Americal created legends around Hill 260 and the hand-to-hand combat in the area of the Torokina River on the island of Bougainville. Sgt. Jessie R. Drowley became the first Americal Medal of Honor recipient for his personal sacrifices during battle.

The division continued to follow the marines around the Pacific, relieving them at Leyte and killing more than four thousand Japanese during extended mop-up operations on the island.

The Americal Division landed in Japan on September 10, 1945, and took part in the occupation of the Yokohama-Kawasaki-Yokosuka area. The division occupied the area until the end of October when the unit was relieved by the First Cavalry Division, and the Americal began preparing for the long-awaited trip home. On December 12, 1945, the battle-scarred Americal was officially inactivated.

In 1967 the Americal Division was reactivated on the island of Oahu and ordered to replace Task Force Oregon in Vietnam's I

Corps. By the time I arrived at Schofield Barracks in October 1967, most of the scheduled training for the 4/3 of the American had been completed. Our days were spent packing boxes with everything from mess hall pots and pans to the 4.2-inch mortar tube, bi-pod, and base plate. In the evenings we retired to the enlisted man (EM) club for one or two too many drinks that made us smart, funny, handsome, and stupid.

Young people from all over America were stealing across the border with Canada in order to avoid the draft. Many others hid behind college, family, or work-related deferments. Anti-war rallies drew thousands across the nation and defiant military-age males burned their Selective Service cards in public as an expression of dissent. I burned my Selective Service card while getting drunk at an EM club on the island of Oahu as a joke just weeks before boarding the USS *General Gordon* for the trip to Vietnam. I was happy to go to Vietnam, but I didn't need the Selective Service card to prove it. Burning my draft card was a violation of rules, but what could they do—send me to Vietnam?

Across the River

05 SEPT. '68—0325H

Weather report: Extremely bad conditions with increased winds and rain. Bad weather may reach a high over the next few days. Take measures to secure property and lives.

The building storm swept up the recon platoon like a straw hut in a hurricane. The platoon was torn apart in a violent display of mortars and automatic weapons. Outnumbered twenty to one, caught in the open, their world was a planet alone. We stood helpless on the other side of the river.

05 SEPT. '68—1140H

Company B is receiving SA (small arms) fire from grid square BS513795. Recon is receiving heavy AW (automatic weapons) fire. Paul Adams was shot then evacuated by C&C, command and control, helicopter in the vicinity of BS545794. Co. C receiving fire from grid BS455579.

05 Sept. '68—1415H

Co. D reports pinned down by AW (automatic weapons) fire from BS474725. Two US were WHA (wounded hostile action).

05 SEPT. '68—1617H

Co. D reports C&C, command and control, ship shot down BS475729.

In the late afternoon of September 6, 1968, Charlie Company was in a large dry field southeast of the horseshoe formed by the

Song Tra Khuc River. Recon platoon was about to run into a deadly shit storm three kilometers north of Company C. The Song Tra Khuc River separated our positions but not our hearts.

06 SEPT. '68—1410H

Recon platoon reports it is pinned down at BS548773.

06 SEPT. '68—1708H

Recon reports 1 US WHA (wounded hostile action), details to follow.

06 SEPT. '68—1725H

A Shark gunship received fire resulting in 2 US WHA; the pilot has been hit.

I distinctly heard the Cobra helicopter gunship pilot say over the battalion frequency, "I have been hit in the leg." The Cobra gunships were new to our unit, and this was the first time I had seen them work. The old helicopter gunships were no more than beefed-up troop transport Huey's with weapons pods attached. The Cobra was only three feet wide and seated a pilot and weapons officer staggered one behind the other. The ship had short wings, called weapons platforms, on each side. They could not carry troops, but they were fast, agile, and heavily armed.

Company C had been receiving small-arms and automatic-weapons fire sporadically from the north side of the Song Tra Khuc, but we were not in the fight. The battalion reconnaissance platoon on the north side of the river was being overrun by a unit possibly twenty times its size.

We could hear the rise and fall of small-arms and automatic-weapons fire. The distinct sound of AK-47s and M16s drew an unpleasant picture of the battle's course. We watched and listened to jets and helicopter gunships make live combat runs all afternoon long. The reconnaissance platoon was within three thousand meters of our position, but we were not allowed to jump the river and get into the fight until the next morning. Higher-higher felt it was too risky to put anything less than a full company into the battle, and the battalion could not gather enough helicopters to lift a hundred troops until the next morning.

After dark, Puff the Magic Dragon came on station. This heavily armed C-130 can put thousands of rounds into a very small area very fast. One in ten rounds is a tracer, but the volume of rounds dispatched gives the appearance of a surreal stairway from heaven or the long red tongue of a fire-breathing dragon washing its enemies away with a casual, flowing lick.

At approximately 10:00 a.m. the next morning, enough choppers came in to lift Charlie Company over the river. Our landing zone for the combat assault was within a hundred meters of the recon battle site from the night before. On the move to the ambush site, I saw one blood trail that led to a bloated, dead military-age Vietnamese male who had flies using his mouth as the doorway to a multiroom luxury hotel. We did not find other blood trails or Vietnamese bodies, but we did find a short section of communication wire.

Alpha Company reached the battle-weary platoon around 3:00 a.m. on September 7, 1968. The casualty reports trickled in for hours. Even though everyone in the Fourth Battalion was involved in this battle, we never talked about it openly either then or later. I know people who served in recon after this date but who had never heard of this battle until I posted it on the battalion website. I am not sure how you learn from mistakes if you don't talk about them.

The status of the reconnaissance platoon as a result of this battle was: ten US KHA (killed hostile action), four US WHA (wounded hostile action), thirteen US uninjured, and one US MIA (missing in action). The following were KHA: Sgt. Secrest, Hanson, Morrow, Moree, Jones (medic), Richards, Still, Williams, and White. The following were WHA: Walker, Gehman, Alerjo, and Montgomery.

07 SEPT. '68—1140H

Co. D request DUSTOFF for 1 US KHA, 4 US WHA result Booby trap at BS564772. William Cooper-KHA, PFC Cheney-WHA, James Elker-WHA, PFC Robert Hannah-WHA.

By the time we crossed the river on the morning of September 7, the battle was over. Alpha Company had reached the reconnaissance platoon at 0300 hours and evacuated the dead and wounded. The rest of recon was pulled out of the field at first light.

I had anticipated seeing men and equipment from the reconnaissance platoon and the NVA scattered around the dry rice paddy battlefield, but I was surprised to find very little. A section of communication wire used to lay landlines was the only evidence we could find that a battle had occurred. The NVA had policed the battlefield with great care. They had even picked up all their brass after/during the battle. The only thing they had left behind were five M16s tied together by their slings with a length of bamboo rope. All five M16s were jammed so tightly you could not kick the chamber open with your foot. They were jammed so tightly that the NVA had decided to discard them and leave them behind.

While we were in the open area where recon had been ambushed, I saw an old water-filled bomb crater left behind by a 250-pound bomb years before. I couldn't help from thinking that the gooks may have thrown weapons, bodies, and/or equipment in the water-filled crater. For all I knew, they had hidden the main street of my hometown at the bottom of that hole. The gooks were good at what they did. I decided to take a look, so I removed all my equipment but left my clothes and boots on. I suspected Charlie may have put punji sticks in the bottom of the crater also, and I was not in the mood to run a sharp piece of bamboo through my body. I got armpit-deep in the water and felt around the bottom of the crater with my feet. I didn't find anything in the hole, but that didn't stop me from thinking that Charlie had concealed the entire Sapper Battalion at the bottom of that water-filled crater.

Charlie Company spent several hours searching the ambush site for anything of interest or value. In the early afternoon, I hooked back up with the Charlie Company command element.

Capt. Middleton was on the horn with the battalion commander who was en route for a face to face. Without removing my rucksack, I dropped to my hands and knees and then rolled over onto my back. The rucksack acted as a backrest that allowed me just enough comfort to close my eyes and doze off while staying alert with my ears.

The battalion commander arrived, dismounted his steel flying horse, and began his conversation with my captain not more than ten feet away from my resting site. They talked about this and that and then got to the meat. Charlie Company would un-ass this position and hump west. Our new mission was to pursue, fix, and destroy the Sapper Battalion. Capt. Middleton finished his part of the conversation with the out-loud thought that he needed to inform First Platoon that they would act as the point element. Without opening my eyes, I told Capt. Middleton that I would deliver the message to them as I rolled onto my stomach, came to my hands and knees, and stood upright under the tremendous weight of my rucksack. I put my helmet on my head and smiled. My steel pot, personalized with symbols and words like many in the company, had a three-inch-high hippie peace sign in ink on the helmet liner's front. I thought the peace symbols worn by heavily armed grunts in the bush were a comical and spirit-lifting combination. Peace and war, war and peace.

"Do you want us to go over the top of the hill or around it?" I asked. There was a short pause before the battalion commander said to go over the top. As I started walking toward First Platoon, I heard the battalion commander say to the captain, "That guy looks like he has been here for a while." That one overheard statement from the battalion commander made me feel proud. He was right; I had been in country for a while and I was just fucked up enough to prove it.

I hooked up with some First Platoon grunts and smoked four pipe loads of weed. When we moved out, I took the point. Busting through a hedgerow, I started across an open field to the west. The hill in front of me was possibly a hundred feet in elevation; it was hard to tell because I couldn't really see the hill. It was more like a lump of vegetation. I could not climb a hill like this. I had to drag myself hand over hand, kicking and clawing until I broke through the top of the vegetation only to repeat the movement a thousand times.

Approximately twenty yards before I reached the mound of vegetation, I heard a scuffle behind me and turned around to check it out. The Murphy twins had dropped their weapons and squared off in the middle of an open field in the middle of a war. I had no idea what the fight was about, but I had three older brothers and understood that things just happen sometimes. This was great. We were chasing a battalion of gooks that had overrun the reconnaissance platoon the night before, and the Murphy twins decided to fight each other. The next guy in line reminded them that we were not back in the world. The twins collected their gear and rejoined the column. Some things are too strange to be true, and other things are too funny not to be true.

For the next two hours, I scratched, clawed, broke through vines, and pulled myself hand over hand up that stinking little hill. The vegetation was so thick that I don't remember seeing the ground. A person must learn to love the jungle. If you try to fight it, your spirit will melt away like ice cream in the hot sun, and at the end of the day the jungle will lap you up as easily as sweet nectar in the beak of a hummingbird. When I reached the top of the hill, I was on the other side of heat exhaustion. My face and arms were covered with bloody sweat from hundreds of vegetation wounds, and I had a tolerable heat-related headache. The next man in line would do what he had to in order to follow me, and after twenty or thirty grunts a trail would start to form. If I tried to use a machete, I would swing until my arm was about to fall off. One of my hands was always occupied with an M16, and I had a rucksack containing my home strapped to my body. The two hours I spent crawling up the hill was a full day's work for most people.

The top of the hill was no more than twenty yards across in any direction. I parked my exhausted and sleep-deprived body on a large boulder and turned the point job over to whoever wanted it. I planned to be the last person off the top of that hill so I could experience what it was like to walk down a path trampled by a hundred people. I knew what it was like to walk point through the jungle, and I needed to find out what it would be like to follow a hundred people through the jungle. After I had walked down the trail stomped in by the company, I decided that point was best for many reasons.

The brass will begin showing up on September 8 to issue their condolences.

08 SEPT. '68—0931H

Major General Getty's Div. Commander arrives at LZ Buff.

08 SEPT. '68—0952H

DG Galloway, Assistant Div. Commander, arrived at LZ Buff.

08 SEPT. 68—1010H

Col. Henderson, Brigade Commander, arrived at LZ Buff.

This citation quote is taken from official national archive files:

THE PRESIDENTIAL UNIT CITATION (ARMY) FOR EX-TRAORDINARY HEROISM TO THE RECONNAISSANCE PLATOON COMPANY E, 4TH BATTALION, 3D INFANTRY 11TH INFANTRY BRIGADE, AMERICAL DIVISION UNITED STATES ARMY

The Reconnaissance Platoon, Company E, 4th Battalion, 3rd Infantry, 11th Light Infantry Brigade distinguished itself by extraordinary heroism in action against a hostile force near the hamlet of Phuoc Loc, Quang Ngai, Republic of Vietnam on 6 and 7 September 1968. The platoon of 27 men was conducting a combat sweep operation on 6 September when it became engaged with a battalion-size enemy force entrenched in fortified defensive positions. Exposed to the heavy automatic weapons and small arms fire from the estimated 400-man enemy force, the men of the Reconnaissance Platoon gallantly fought against the numerical odds and established defensive perimeters. Maintaining their position integrity, men of the platoon, with complete disregard for their own safety, braved the heavy fire to bring their fallen comrades within the perimeter. Although under heavy fire and repeated attacks from the enemy, the men of the Reconnaissance Platoon valorously held their positions, directed airstrikes and artillery fire on the enemy.

Positions and repulsed all enemy efforts to overrun their defenses. The platoon was able to engage the enemy force until reinforcements arrived during the early morning hours of 7 September. A sweep of the battlefield on the morning of 7 September revealed that the Reconnaissance Platoon had killed 48 enemy soldiers. Intelligence from captured prisoners indicated that the enemy force had suffered 88 casualties, rendering it ineffective as a fighting force. The Reconnaissance Platoon is credited with spoiling an impending attack on the city of Quang Ngai by discovering and inflicting heavy losses on one of the key enemy forces poised for attack, thereby sparing free world forces and the population of the city of Quang Ngai much loss of life, equipment and personal property. The heroic actions of the men in the platoon aided in the defeat of major enemy forces which had been poised for attacks on the major cities of Quang Ngai province. The gallantry and devotion to duty of the men of the Reconnaissance Platoon, against numerically superior enemy forces, are in keeping with the highest traditions of the United States Army and reflect great credit upon themselves and the Armed Forces of the United States.

What the Presidential Unit Citation does not say is that the 4/3 had spent from July 3 to September 4 in an AO (area of operation) a hundred miles to the north of LZ Buff. We had just returned to the LZ Buff AO on September 4. On September 5, 1968, Alpha, Bravo, and Charlie companies conducted combat assaults into the LZ Buff AO. On September 4 the reconnaissance platoon and Delta Company were repositioned to the top of the LZ Buff firebase.

I became depressed after our reconnaissance platoon was overrun. My system reeked with poisons from the toxic rice paddies and constantly bleeding leech-infested cuts from the elephant grass and jungle vegetation. Once I received a grass cut at the base of my nose, and a week later my top lip was infected to the point that if I touched it blood would flow. I think it was jungle rot. The medic fixed me up with some cream and I stayed in the bush. I was sick, dangerous, and insane. For more than a month, my stomach would not keep anything down except C ration chicken noodle soup heated with a small piece of plastic explosive and eaten from the can. I had been transformed from a veteran to a lighted fuse capable of blowing up at any minute. A look into my eyes found only silent depth, dancing with rage and running to the front of the fucked-up-beyond-all-recognition line.

At the end of a day's march, I would rejoin the command group to help construct a fighting position. The company commander sometimes noticed me as I returned to the command group after a day's march. I believe he used me as a scale to determine when to order up new clothes for the troops. I would join the command group wearing shirts and pants that were ripped to shreds. My boot soles would sometimes be flapping when I walked, and sweat mixed with my own blood would cover my arms, neck, and face.

The blood was from the 99 percent. I believe that there are 1,000 different types of vegetation in Vietnam. Of these, 999 species will poke, cut, scratch, trip, hitchhike, and act as leech highways. The other 1 percent is deadly poisonous. No matter what we did, the jungle would have our blood.

Many times we barely had enough food, water, and fully equipped men, but we could call in artillery, gunships, jets, B-52s, and sixteen-inch battleship rounds to bring damn-damn to a grid coordinates on demand.

The company had remained overnight on top of a low jungle-surrounded hill. The next morning we came off the hill and were patrolling along a dry riverbed with dense jungle in all directions. I was traveling with the point element when we received sniper fire directed at the command group that was in the center of the column. The sniper had shot the CO's radio telephone operator in the stomach resulting in the entire company going to ground. One sniper shot could hold up the whole company for a long period of time. I was frustrated and pissed, so I put a magazine into the closest tree line. As I was changing magazines redesignated, a rookie butter bar, second lieutenant, crawled over to me and asked in an excited voice what I was shooting at. I told the officer that I wasn't shooting at anything except the fucking tree line. I was tired of the gooks putting us to ground and I needed to blow off some steam.

The lieutenant quickly put his entire platoon, approximately thirty grunts, on line and started pumping lead into the tree line. I dumped another magazine into the trees and when I rolled over to reload, I saw a helicopter gunship releasing rockets from his stable gun position at about two hundred meters in range and three hundred feet in elevation. The rockets looked like they were headed straight at me, and I hoped the pilot knew what he was doing. The rockets slammed into the same tree line that was receiving a platoon's worth of small-arms fire. The gunship made a couple more runs before returning to base to reload. My impulsive dumping of a magazine into the tree line had been followed by the platoon and then the helicopter gunship. All in all, I spent a lot of taxpayers' dollars this day just to blow off some steam. We were short of clothes, water, and other equipment, but we could bring in damn-damn from the air or from the sea onto a bunch of trees.

The helicopter gunship left station to rearm and refit. The rookie lieutenant tried to recruit me and two people from his platoon to run an unauthorized, unplanned recon that would have us separated from the rest of the company and any sanity this war could offer. I baulked at the plan. This guy was a platoon leader who planned to leave his platoon behind while he ran a risky solo recon without telling the company commander. Didn't he know that whenever we tried to chase Charlie like this, there was always a well-planned ambush nearby? The platoon leader should have spent the time taking care of his men instead of hunting glory for his actions. This is another reason green lieutenants don't last very long in combat. A friend who was a medic for the Ninth Infantry Division in Vietnam said their lieutenants lasted only about two weeks. Granted, the Ninth Infantry Division was in a different area of operation and suffered many more KIA than we did, but rookie butter bars were no less dangerous.

The Freedom Bird

In October 1968 I got a punji stick in my left knee while conducting a combat assault with Charlie Company. A punji stick is a piece of bamboo sharpened at both ends and stuck in the ground. The exposed point may be dipped in human feces for greater effect. I found the punji stick by the large gray moss- and debris-covered rock that I was hiding behind.

I was hiding behind the rock because that's what I always did when I reached the destination of a combat assault. I would get off the chopper and hide behind a rock or a tree. I could hide behind a chick dressed up like a rice paddy dike on a motorcycle, and I had learned to conceal my entire body behind a distant sound or a single blade of grass. I was determined to hide behind something because that's how the army had trained me. They called it cover and concealment.

Even though I was a self-proclaimed expert at hiding, I always liked to be on the first lift of a combat assault. All those choppers flying in close formation in a pack scared the hell out of me, so it made sense to jump the first bird in line whenever I could. I will never understand why the choppers flew so close in formation. A mistake or enemy fire could start a series of events I didn't want to be a part of.

This particular combat assault was preceded by two B-52s dropping half their load in the target valley. The B-52s executed a

180-degree turn and dropped the rest of their load before departing. Both Company C and Company D were far enough away to be safe but close enough to be impressed. We could feel the shaking of the earth like God taking command of the planet with a completely controlling hand and shaking it. The sound was a deep, deep rumble unlike the sharp smacking sound of artillery or the air-moving freight train sound of sixteen-inch rounds from the Battleship *Missouri* as they passed overhead. This sound was god-awful death from forty thousand feet. Hundreds of bombs went individually and combined into one move-the-earth rumble.

Within minutes after the god-awful death from above subsided, we heard the wop-wop-wop of helicopters descending on our dry rice paddy LZ. Some of the choppers picked up the first lift of Charlie Company and took us to the west ridge of the valley. That's how I got behind this large gray moss- and debris-covered rock.

So I hid behind this large gray rock after a combat assault and got a punji stick in my left knee. I called the second lift and tried to send the message about punji sticks. It's hard to talk on an open mike inside a heavily loaded chopper in flight. I don't know if the message was copied by the following lifts, but no one else, to the best of my knowledge, got stuck that day.

I saw what used to be a human very close to my hide rock. The body was five meters from the edge of a crater created by a 250-pound high-explosive bomb. Pulverized ashes might better describe the condition of the remains. He was burned into the ground by hot concussion and shrapnel, like a surreal sculpture hinting at the life that used to exist there shortly before we arrived.

I was like, "What's up, Dude? You want a smoke?" A dropped cigarette would poke a hole through his body like a sharp spear.

I was like, "I think you're looking thin, Dude. Maybe you need to stop smoking." He was smoking from the heat of the B-52 bombs.

We patrolled the ridge and on the third day worked our way to the bottom of the valley. At this point my left knee had swollen up real good from the punji stick, and a medic told me to go to a firebase to get it fixed.

At the bottom of the valley, I would have an excellent front row seat for a show where fast movers, jets, were dropping napalm close enough for us to feel the heat. A pull me–push me FAC (forward air control) plane was on station using WP (white phosphorus) to mark targets for the fast movers and a gook-piloted heavily armed single propeller Cessna that could slide into box canyons and other tight places the fast mover could not reach.

I think the battalion CO's chopper was shot down this week. If memory serves, he was shot down three times in one week. This did not bother me much. Every time he flew over our location, the chopper told Charlie where we were. After he was shot down, I sent an imaginary thank-you note to the gooks and told them I had always dreamed of shooting down a chopper with my M16. We would live in the bush for a month eating C rats and sleeping with leeches while the chopper heads would fly over our location for six minutes and head for base to drink cold beer, boom-boom party girls, and sleep in a bed with clean sheets. Dustoff choppers and their crews were exempt from all criticism because God was their pilot.

Later that day, after I'd fantasy-airmailed my note, we prepared for another combat assault. Choppers came in, and we were lifted out of the valley floor to the top of the eastern ridge. I was on the first chopper of the first lift. When the chopper was about six feet off the ground, I jumped, much to the dismay of the pilot. I can read lips well enough to know that the pilot was not praising my courage and tumbling skills. No, it was more like, "You dumb SOB! What the fuck are you doing?"

After the company had landed and formed a perimeter, I talked with the captain about catching a ride to an LZ to get my wound treated. He knew I had never skipped out or ghosted during ten months in country. I was there even when I didn't have to be. The CO said that if I could bum a ride on the battalion commander's bird, it would be OK with him.

The battalion commander landed his chopper to confer with the company CO. I ran up to the battalion CO stinking from beaucoup sweat and no personal hygiene for over a week plus the fact that I had not worn shorts for more than nine months.

Shorts will kill you. The first day of an extended patrol in tropical country the killer shorts will chafe the legs. The chafe turns into open sores on day two. On day three the open sores become infected as you're wading through waist-deep rice paddies or, as we called them, open public sewers. On day four you might as well pack your shit because a dustoff is going to take you to the rear with the folks who have the gear.

In the same light, shoestrings will save your life. I tied shoestrings around my legs above the calves to keep the leeches lower. I replaced the sling on my M16 with shoestrings because the sling was too noisy and in the wrong place. I used shoestrings to tie on the soles of my boots when they came apart in the jungle. Shoestrings were used to tie a poncho to bamboo stakes and pegs that supported my hooch for the night or shade for the day. We used shoestrings to tie the PRC-25 radio mike close to our ear so only we could hear. Shoestrings secured my socks to the outside of a rucksack so they would air out while I marched during the day. Shoestrings could make splints and slings. The strings that kept the grunts alive existed only because the black market found no profit in them.

I approached the battalion commander and dropped my pants to my ankles to show proof of the wound. Looking back on it forty years later, I think this is when I concluded that the battalion CO was not gay for unwashed grunts with an M16 in their hands and their pants around their ankles.

I requested a ride to whatever LZ he was going to. After looking at my leg, the battalion CO agreed I should have the wound treated. I did not tell the colonel about my note to the gooks.

After this ride I would never again be required to go on patrol or to the field. This was a good thing. The helicopter dropped me off at Duc Pho. The first sergeant from Echo Company met me at the chopper and told me to go to the medics. "Get fixed up and tell them you have earned a Purple Heart," he said.

Having just come out of the bush, I was still armed and angry. My scent alone would have made most people seek cover. The first sergeant did not attempt to piss me off. Tears began streaming down my face. In an emotionally filled dangerous outburst, I informed the first sergeant that everyone in Charlie Company was losing their legs and arms and their lives, and the only fucking thing they received was a Purple Heart. I pointed out a dark place where the sun didn't shine and told him to put the Purple Heart there. I was out of control.

When I visited the medic tent, they also told me I had earned a Purple Heart. In my mind, medics walk on water, so I told them in a civil voice that I didn't want a Purple Heart because my mom would receive a telegram notifying her of the wound and that would concern her. I told the medics I would be home in two months and could tell her about the punji stick then.

They said, "OK, but you will be sorry." Twenty-five years later when I started dealing with the VA, I found out the medics were right. I told you medics walk on water and now you have proof, because who else can predict the future?

For the next two months I smoked weed. I smoked like the top of a nuclear reactor's cooling tower. I bought a brand-new pipe and burned a hole through it in a month. One day I smoked twenty joints before lunch, ate, and then smoked my pipe for the rest of the day. I do not remember ever being stoned. I suppose not remembering is a sure indication that I was stoned.

Smoke could not match the full-combat alert that my mind and body were in. Even after being out of the field for close to two months, my hyper personality and combat experience had me wired, violent, depressed, and—I would find out later—a bunch of other emotional and psychological stuff I had not even heard of.

During the last week of November, I was handed my ticket back to the world. I went to Chu Lai and just waited. This was semi morbid because I was waiting for dead guys. I couldn't remember any names, but I couldn't forget the explosive body-ripping images of people being blown up by a Bouncing Betty. I could have jumped on a plane and flown to Cam Ranh Bay, but I needed to know. I wanted to see how many Charlie Company boys would show up. After five days it was clear I was on a flawed mission. Some of the boys had been wounded, some had finished their time in the service, some had transferred or extended. I had only my memories devoid of the names that went with them.

When it was time to go home, I caught a flight to Cam Ranh Bay. As the C-130 was about five minutes from the destination runway, I saw smoke coming from the electrical panel. I was about to inhale the smoke but decided I might someday want to run for political office, or not.

Everyone in the cargo department was asleep except for me. I went to the back ramp where the crew chief was catching Zs and gently woke him. He startled awake and looked at me with contempt in his eyes. C-130s are loud with big gaping holes along the back ramp with the wind screaming by. There was too much noise to yell, so I stepped to the side and pointed to the smoking electrical panel just behind the pilot's cabin.

At this point the crew chief became the leader of all the panic that would visit the C-130 over the next five minutes. The crew chief jumped up to run to the front of the plane where the smoke was as he contacted the pilot on his headphone setup. His cord got tangled up and unplugged before it broke. He had to come back and plug it in causing additional disturbance, which woke up and alerted more people on the flight to our crisis.

The crew chief was in charge and aggressively recruiting sleep-deprived partners for the growing panic on the plane. Although panic is an understandable result of being trapped on a burning C-130 in flight, it does not solve the problem. We were still in the air, and the electrical panel was still smoking.

When we landed, the passengers were lined up tightly behind the side door I had been sitting beside when I first noticed the smoke. Everyone wanted to be the first out of the plane. I think six guys were in my old seat. I stayed the last in line figuring I would have soft, injured bodies to land on.

I timed our landing from when our tires first touched the ground until we stopped, got off, and firemen in silver suits were getting on the plane with hoses. The short-run touchdown and evacuation took less than thirty seconds. When my feet touched the tarmac, I walked away from the C-130 and never looked back. I did not know or care what happened to the plane.

The freedom bird people signed me in and said I would be on the first flight the next day. About one month earlier, I had put a ten-pack of Nuc Maos in my wallet with the intent of taking them back to the world. Nuc Maos are named after the village they were made in. They were Pall Mall–size prerolled joints that came in a pack of ten for $1.50. I was concerned about being searched getting on or off the plane, so I went to the beach and smoked every last one of them. It was a mission. Not to get stoned but to get home.

The USO or other people who do these kinds of things organized a party for the departing veterans inside a large building with bright lights. You would think light radiates outward, but in this case I saw it as a big fucking magnet attracting every unpinned grenade in this tropical jungle kingdom. The building was like the headquarters of the galactic solar exchange. Nobody needs that much light for anything. They could cover up a black hole and have light left over. The light was strong enough to hold up the ceiling without need for the walls.

The biscuit bitches, USO girls, hosting the party provided food, music, entertainment, and nonalcoholic drinks for the homeward-bound veterans. Three times I made it to the door and looked in at the REMFs (rear area mother fuckers) smiling and telling lies about their imaginary "cop a feel" from a round-eyed Donut Dolly who was also called a USO girl. The doorway, the line between light and dark, was like the concertina wire that separated an LZ from the bush. Once I stepped into the light, once I crossed that wire, Charlie would have the upper hand. If Charlie hung around after first contact, we would fuck him up. But Charlie was smart. He would hit and run, or place a mine and i *nhanh* (go fast). He rarely presented a target.

In my high school yearbook, I am listed as the outstanding male personality of the senior class of 1966. Less than three years later,

I was the king of paranoia and antisocial behavior who couldn't attend a party on his own behalf. Throughout my youth I had received complements from adults for never using colorful language. Two years in the military and a combat tour had turned my vocabulary into a string of foul words. Sometimes "fuck" was the only word I would say for three sentences in a row. This one-word fetish solved a lot of my spelling problems. I had become a man who could cuss but not write.

Later in life I would drop into my most vulgar vocabulary when in the company of the self-proclaimed saved who believe that they have somehow achieved a position closer to God than mine. They claim that they are doing God's work as if God were incompetent and incapable of doing his own work. These people want to save themselves by crawling up my ass and getting between me and God. They don't understand that my God has no need for hell or the devil and any of the man-sponsored fears. The conditions were invented by man and were designed to frighten people into compliance. My God is loving, all knowing, and everlasting. The already-saved don't care that I have a great relationship with God. God tells me that I am an asshole, and I remind God that I was created in his image. We both laugh and skip down the road holding hands. Some would suggest that laughing, holding hands, and skipping down the road with God makes us gay. So, what if we are gay?

I had an aisle seat on the flight back to the world at the end of November 1968. As the plane lifted off Vietnamese soil, I reached across the chest of the person in the window seat and flipped off the entire fucking country. When we landed at McChord Air Force Base in Washington State, everyone clapped. Four hours later I was out of the army and hopping a plane to Portland. My brother and sister-in-law picked me up at the airport. They gave me dinner and a piece of floor to sleep on. I ran patrols all night long.

The next day I called my mother to check in. She told me that my best friend from high school was in Portland being fitted for his prosthetic arm. We had played football and basketball together. We spent every weekend together. We took basic training in Fort Lewis, Washington, together. He went to Fort Polk, Louisiana, for jungle training and then joined the Big Red One, where he became a squad leader. After running patrols for nine months, he lost his right arm in a nighttime battle.

As luck would have it, I hooked up with my high school best friend the next day. Late that night we were at a bar and grill in downtown Portland when a homeless drunk told me to go get a haircut. I blew my top. My buddy helped calm me down. I told the drunk that I hadn't killed anyone in a long time but would make an exception in his case. This was sort of a lie as I maintain I never killed anyone. I told him that forty hours ago I was in Vietnam finishing my one-year tour, and I didn't remember seeing his sorry ass in my foxhole. I had spent 362 days in a shit hole that was beginning to make more sense than the civilians back in the world who never showed up.

Less than forty hours out of Vietnam and I was psyched to kill a civilian for little reason. I did not know that this kind of anger and hate would be with me for the rest of my life.

If you have ever known the feeling of returning from war to a grateful nation waving flags, offering kisses, and heaping tons of love on its returning veterans, then you and I have not experienced the same thing. Within one hour of receiving my discharge papers from the army, I called a cab to take me to the Sea-Tac, Seattle-Tacoma airport. The cab driver ripped me off by charging over one hundred dollars for a thirty-dollar ride. God bless America.

I purchased a ticket to Portland and retreated to the restroom to get out of my dress blues and into some civilian clothes. The military clothes made me a target for looks of contempt and muted slurs from long-haired hippies. I had heard about the possibility of being called names when I got home from Vietnam, so I planned a response. If someone called me a baby killer, I was going to say, "Don't forget the rape, murder, and mutilation of unarmed civilians. We do that all the time too." The hippies would never know I was speaking the truth.

The second possible source of conflict was the hollow, "Thank you for serving our nation." This comment pissed me off and usually came from loudmouthed no-shows who never sacrificed one minute of their lives for America. These people could not wait to buy a flag and send others off to die in some leech-infested shit hole, but they seldom showed up themselves. I personally didn't know how invading a country that posed no threat to the United States would serve our nation. Once dressed in civilian clothes, I became just another one of them. The civilians accepted me with smiles and a nod devoid of judgment from either left or right. Clothes do make a difference, and so do hand grenades.

After a few days in Portland, I caught a flight to Boise, Idaho, where two years earlier I had stood at attention for the first time in my life to take the oath of service and officially become a part of the nation's military. My reasons for flying to Boise could have been to thank the people at the induction center who helped me have such a wonderful experience in the military and beautiful Southeast Asia, but it wasn't.

My brother was a deputy sheriff in Malheur County, Oregon, which was only a hundred miles from the Boise airport. He picked me up and let me stay at his place. The next day I borrowed his car and drove back to Boise, where I got a room for the night. In the early evening I drove to the Idaho State University dormitories to see my ex-girlfriend.

This young lady was the love of my life. That is why I broke up with her after receiving my orders for Vietnam. She was the love of my life, and I was sure I would die in Vietnam. To keep from hurting her, I asked for my class ring back. This went over real well with her as she loved me also. I was unable to tell her the full truth and explained our breakup as an effort to give her the freedom to date others while I was gone. I didn't tell her I thought I would die in Vietnam.

Waiting in the dorm lobby for her to return gave me the opportunity to look at the faces of the young students. I say "young," but truthfully we were the same age in years but not experience. I was the twenty-one-year-old man who had died from drinking rigor mortis tea, and they were the twenty-one-year-old kids about ready to start their lives. We did not have much in common. They were excited about the prospects for the rest of their lives, and I was lost in the jungle counting my dead.

My high school love returned to the dormitory on the arm of another man. I waited while she finished her dance before making my presence known. I had told her to date others, and she was beautiful. I held no blame, but I knew it was over between us. Before this we had been an exclusive item, and now I was the third wheel. There were worse things in life.

We sat in the dormitory parking lot talking. She asked me where I wanted to go, and to my surprise I said, "Your church." This surprised her also as I had never been much of a church person before. We drove to the Catholic Church a few blocks away. She instructed me in church etiquette as we stood just inside the door. When she got to the part about lighting candles, I grew interested. I asked if the candles had to be for dead people and she said no. I asked her how many candles I could light and she said, "As many as you like."

I started lighting candles and counting the dead. "This one is for you," I would say as I lit a candle for the Vietnamese female who was raped by the three grunts. "This one is for you," I would say as I lit a candle for the two unarmed Vietnamese males we killed in the canoe. "This one is for you," I would say as I lit a candle for the mutilated body of John-John. I would say, "This one is for you... and you...and you..." until tears began streaming down my face and I became concerned about setting the church on fire with all the candles I needed to light. I lit one last candle for everybody and put my overheated lighter away.

My love and I were like two cars on the freeway going in opposite directions. Now I see you, now I don't. She deserved love, happiness, and security. I wanted to end the war and slap the American public in the face for killing my veterans for monetary gain. Her life held the hope of children and success while my life had ended months before, leaving behind a zombie dominated with bitter hate and deep-seated revenge fantasies.

A fifteen-month-long circle was about to be completed as my brother drove me to my parents' home in Harney County, Oregon, on his first day off work. I had written him a letter just before deployment to Vietnam. The letter contained instructions about how to distribute the insurance money should I die in a combat zone. I had earmarked most of the money for my parents. The remaining sum was to be distributed evenly between my five siblings. A letter written fifteen months before could now be torn up and burned in the trash.

The duffel bag containing all I owned was carried into the house for me. This was the first and last time anyone would do that. I had never been stronger in my life, and yet the family chose this moment to help me. The little pleasures are always so sweet.

Two months before the freedom bird brought me back to the world; I bought an Akai reel-to-reel tape recorder at the Chu Lai Post Exchange. The price was unbeatable in Vietnam, and the shipping would be done directly from the manufacturer. I had also sent my mother two Asian-dressed dolls I hoped she would add to the ones my oldest brother had sent her from Japan many years before.

After both my parents had gone to work on my first day home, I turned my attention to unpacking the gifts I had sent. I unpacked the Akai recorder with a lot of excitement. This was the most money I had ever spent on anything, and I had no clue what I would do if it were broken or missing. I was not disappointed. The recorder was outstanding. I still have it to this day.

It doesn't work, but I still have it. The model I had purchased would play six-inch reel-to-reel tapes, plus it had the ability to play and record eight-track tapes. At the time, 1969, eight-track tapes were in everyone's car. If this dates me, I don't mind—because the alternative to growing old is to die. I don't have an excessive love for life, but that doesn't mean I want to die. Dying is easy; it is life that is hard.

The two dolls I had sent my mom were wrapped in a package marked "Do not open till Xmas." At the time I sent the package, I felt sure I would be home before that date. I opened the box carefully so as not to damage the dolls. They were in perfect shape, and I was sure my mother would like them as much as the Japanese dolls she had displayed in our living room for years. I ripped the head off of one of the Vietnamese dolls and dumped its contents into a plastic bag. The sweet smell of Asian weed filled my nose.

I cleaned up both dolls, put their heads back on, and set them on the counter so my mother would see them when she finished work that day. I hoped she would enjoy them. I knew I would because I had just bought a new pipe downtown and was in the process of breaking it in.

Within two weeks I received a job offer to feed cattle on a ranch in Diamond Valley. The boss's son, nicknamed Luke, liked my

Asian weed and would soon come to like my hard work. I was told to report for duty after the holiday season. It seems to me that much of my life has been charmed. I have received almost everything I have asked for. Many times I got more than I anticipated, but I knew God had his plans also and I would have to take the good with the better. An example of this would be that I wanted to go to war to learn about life. God sent me to war to learn about trauma so I could coach others. I got what I wanted, and so did God.

Feeding cattle in the winter is a lot like living outside the wire in a combat zone. You must complete the mission every day without regard to weather, terrain, and anything else beyond human control. I could control the clothes I wore, the equipment I used, and the attitude I showed up to work with. I could not control the weather, and cattle had to be fed every day. The only option was to complete the mission.

While working for Luke's father, I coached Luke about how to avoid the draft. We became good friends. We bought a kilo of weed in 1968 for $140. The value of that kilo on the street was about $650 at the time. The street value of that same kilo today would be close to $9,000. Neither he nor I wanted to sell weed, but we both smoked like the stack of a steam locomotive climbing uphill. Luke could roll a joint with one hand while riding his horse, and I could smoke them as fast as he could roll.

We rode horses, fed cattle, operated tractors for clearing and leveling land, and got stoned. Luke took me to Nevada one weekend and fed me acid. I liked hallucinations: they were fun, colorful, and 100 percent better than the Vietnam-generated nightmares and flashbacks that tracked me day and night.

Living on a ranch forty miles out of town kept me out of trouble with my family and the law. On the weekends we would go into town to party. I ran into the same thing other combat veterans have gone through since the beginning of war. Someone would ask a question about Vietnam and as soon as I started to respond, they would turn their backs and walk away. They didn't want to know the truth; they just wanted to judge me. Most times they had made the judgment before we ever spoke.

In late spring the Diamond Ranch didn't need me anymore, so I went to work for the BLM (Bureau of Land Management) on a firefighting crew. This particular fire season was not very impressive. I think I went on fewer than ten fires the whole season. The fires we did get were much bigger after we arrived than they were before we got there. Bigger fires meant more hours and bigger checks. The ground we let burn was covered with sagebrush. Once the sagebrush was burned off, the ground could be planted with grass seed for cattle and wildlife.

The story about the My Lai massacre broke in November of 1969. The civilians around me seemed shocked to learn that a nineteen year old American boy could rape, murder and mutilate unarmed civilians. I was surprised that the civilians were shocked. I could list off six different times when the people I was on patrol with killed unarmed gooks. What American civilians were shocked at was no more than standard operating procedure (SOP) in my evaluation.

The Farm

Come on all you brave young men
Uncle Sam needs your help again
He got himself in a terrible jam
Way down yonder in Vietnam
Lyrics by; Country Joe McDonald;
From the song, the fish cheer

In the summer of 1969, my best friend from Echo Company's mortar platoon, B. W., began sending me letters listing nineteen different bands that were planning to hold a massive rock concert on Max Yasgur's six-hundred-acre farm in the Catskills of New York state.

I had never attended a rock concert before, and this one sounded like it would serve the purpose. I cashed in the remaining savings bonds the military had twisted my arm to buy and got a fresh haircut, which was a mistake. I collected a local sampling of acid, mescaline, hash, and pot to entertain my friends in Virginia.

B. W. met me at Dulles International Airport, IAD, in Washington, DC. B. W. had been a squad leader for one of our four-deuce mortars in 1968. We were joined by Jim, who acted as my RTO (radio telephone operator) in the field for a time before becoming a forward observer for Delta Company.

B. W. and his girlfriend joined Jim and me in the Volkswagen van for the drive to New York State. We were very generous at offering rides to long-haired hitchhikers along the road. By the time we got within ten miles of the Woodstock stage, both lanes of the country road were filled with vehicles going the same direction. It took us three more hours to get within a mile of the stage, where we pulled the van into a meadow that looked like a good place to set up camp. When we opened the door of our magic van at the Woodstock camping site, a dozen people rolled out.

Woodstock became the number one coolest item on my growing list of significant historical events that I had been a part of. Another number one on my list of "been there and done that" was the Vietnam War.

No one in our group had purchased tickets to the concert beforehand. Our first task was to walk the mile to the main gate in the hopes of securing tickets to the event. I never did make it all the way to the main gate as every time I walked the trail around the outside of the ten-foot-high cyclone fence surrounding the concert area, I would see two to three hundred people throw their combined body weight against the fence and knock it over. Thousands of people would then rush through the breach in the festival perimeter.

This was an eye-opening event for someone like me, who was so naive I had gotten a high and tight haircut before making the trip to New York. Some people were walking around naked; others were holding signs above their heads that said "Acid $0.75." The walking police patrols were surrounded by pot-smoking, stoned, naked women offering their bodies to the men in uniform. The police had their act together for this event. They concerned themselves with violence and other serious crimes while taking no interest in people smoking pot or tripping on acid unless the person involved posed a hazard to themselves or others.

Janis Joplin sang "Ball and Chain" with Jefferson Airplane while she threw down shots of whiskey to numb her vocal chords. Country Joe and the Fish thrilled me with "Alice's Restaurant" and the "Fish Cheer." Sly and the Family Stone entertained us, while the Who took it to another level with the rock opera "Tommy."

We left the concert on Sunday in order to beat the rush. B. W. had offered to drive Jim and me home. Jim lived in Kansas and I lived in Oregon. These were illuminating, expansive, and educational times for a person like me, who had been raised in a small town with a population of four hundred if you counted the kids and dogs. One Sunday I was at Max Yasgur's farm listening to all the best modern rock bands with two war buddies and four hundred thousand hippies, the next Sunday B. W. and I were standing at the nine-thousand-foot elevation point at the head of the Kiger Gorge box canyon on the top of Steens Mountain Wilderness area in Eastern Oregon.

Woodstock helped me resolve some of the confusion generated by Vietnam. Many Americans claimed that we were the best country in the history of the world, and yet the war crimes I had witnessed told me there was room for doubt.

In February 1968, as part of the annual Tet Offensive, the Communists of North Vietnam massacred as many as three thousand Vietnamese civilians and threw them in a ditch near the city of Hue. Less than three weeks later, the Eleventh Light Infantry Brigade's Task Force Barker massacred between three hundred and five hundred civilians and threw them in a ditch beside the village of My Lai. The only difference between the two events as far as I could see was the size of the ditch and how many bodies it took to fill it.

I reject apologists who rant that the commies killed more than we did so we must somehow be superior. Bullshit. If you kill one or you kill a hundred unarmed civilians, it is no less a war crime. Each human killed had someone they loved and were loved by. You can massacre twenty or two hundred and it is still a crime against humanity, the Uniform Code of Military Justice, and God.

While still in Vietnam I had made a promise to my dead that I would do as much as I could to end the war if I made it out alive. My heart steeled the barricades of this commitment. I had no choice in the matter. I had planned to become part of the anti-war movement before the Woodstock concert, and millions of hippies represented by the people on the farm did everything to support my contentions. This former grunt, the angry outrider with a fresh haircut, would become a long-haired Vietnam veteran advocating for peace. My mind and concern for humanity said: wrong war, wrong time, and wrong place.

The trip west with my friends was a one-of-a-kind journey. We stopped or took detours whenever we agreed to explore something of interest. We went hundreds of miles out of our way just to eat lunch at a place in Kansas that championed itself as the exact geographical center of the United States. We dropped Jim off at his parents' home in the Midwest and spent the night there. The next day B. W., his girlfriend, and I continued our excursion west.

The terrain and weather throughout Middle America greeted me like a smiling stranger. I had never made the trip overland before. I had no idea this beautiful landscape and weather existed anywhere in the United States. Words, pictures, and books allowed only a brief glimpse of the possibilities, but they could never have told the complete story of the Midwest anyway.

The highways along the rolling plains of Kansas appeared endless. Some named mountains would be little more than anonymous foothills in eastern Oregon, where I would leave this long-haired band of Woodstock veterans.

Looking at the rows of nearly ripe yellow corn for miles on end brought a question to mind. There was something missing, and I couldn't put it in place. The missing element dawned on me as we traversed Nebraska. Irrigation ditches. That's what was missing. The irrigation ditches and/or circular irrigation sprinkler systems necessary to grow crops in Eastern Oregon were nowhere to be seen in the former dust bowls of the American heartland. I would find out later that Iowa and other Midwest states received so much rain that they had to install special drain systems to keep their crops from flooding.

Clouds would appear dark, low, and slow on the horizon. Clouds at a distance could be outrun by our magic van heading for a new land with three strong and alive twenty-one-year-olds who were about to carve out an existence of their combined shared experiences. It felt like springtime near the spot of creation.

We took fun and active pictures at every new state line sign and danced on the steps of the Boise state capitol. We wanted to make up for having missed the 1968 year of love. B. W. and I had paid our dues by sacrificing two years of our lives in the military. We wanted all the nation had to offer including drugs, sex, and rock and roll. We may not have gotten it all, but we at least sampled everything on the plate once.

In the southeast corner of Oregon, there is a 428,156-acre piece of public BLM land called the Steens Mountain Wilderness. Informational brochures for this area boast that the location is as far as you can get from any populated place in the lower forty-eight United States. The 150-mile-long and 50-mile-wide geographical anomaly rises from a 4,000-foot-high lava plain on its west face to a peak at the 9,600-foot-elevation before crashing vertically to 4,000 feet in elevation, Alvord Desert on its east flank of the wilderness. Standing on the 9,600-foot summit allows the viewer to see

Oregon, Idaho, Nevada, and California from the same spot on a clear day. B. W. threw a rock off the Kiger Gorge box canyon that did not touch ground until it dropped nearly 5,000 feet in elevation.

B. W. and I had traveled from peace to war aboard the USS *General Gordon* across the Pacific Ocean. We had flown separately from war back to the world on a freedom bird destined for our families. We had driven a VW van from Woodstock where thousands of half-naked, all-stoned hippies on a grass-covered hill in New York state sang about giving peace a chance. We camped in a wilderness as far away from population as you can get in the lower forty-eight. I heard rumors that on this day nineteen people had dropped acid at the head of Kiger Gorge in the Steens Mountain Wilderness area. I was there all day and only remember counting eighteen other stoned people.

When I suggested to B. W. and his gal that we go to the Steens Mountain, I promised them that it was a place they could yell as loud as they wanted and no one would hear them. As it turned out, all nineteen people at this magnificent spot could yell until our tongues fell off and no one would hear us.

The summer of 1969 was beginning to leave behind a scorching hot August as B. W. continued his journey to the West Coast. I finished up my summer employment and prepared to establish a new area of operation in a small college town in Southern Oregon.

On a Sunday evening in September 1969, one week before school started, I packed my Akai tape recorder, music, and clothes into a Mercury Cougar for the all-night drive to Ashland, Oregon. While growing up I had never planned to go to college. In high school we were required to take standard achievement tests during our sophomore and senior years. I scored exactly the same number of points both times I took the test. The school guidance counselor called me in for a face-to-face. He noted that I had identical scores on both tests; he commented that he had never seen anything like it before and was wondering if I knew how this could happen. I told him I had done it with patterns. I never read any of the questions. I filled in the answer boxes by forming patterns. The thing that surprised me most was that the patterns resulted in identical scores even though the tests were two years apart.

I did not attend college for the purpose of acquiring a degree. My mission was to protest the war, and if I accidentally learned something along the way then so be it. I was angry and bitter at a nation that proclaimed itself the best in the world but had demonstrated to me that they were sometimes no more than armed bullies and thugs who sent others to sacrifice and die while they pumped themselves up with hot air to stay elevated above the truth.

My GPA coming out of high school was 1.4. I think I registered for college with an X as my signature. I was allowed to stay on campus because of a policy that exempted veterans from the GPA requirements that other nonveterans faced. The rule stipulated that veterans could attend college for one term regardless of their high school GPA.

This rule was made for me. I did well enough to stay in school after the first term. By the end of my third term at Southern Oregon College, I had made the dean's list. This told me I wasn't stupid; I was just uninterested in anything that was not sports, grabass, and spitball at the high school level.

I arrived in Ashland at 4:00 a.m. and pulled into the only open restaurant in town for coffee and breakfast. As I was looking through the local paper for a place to rent, the only other patron got my attention and announced he had an apartment he was willing to rent for fifty dollars a month. That was perfect, as my total wealth at the time was $150 in cash and 00000 in my checking account. I had planned on using the GI Bill to finance my anti-war mood.

The day was spent registering for school, signing up for the GI Bill, and checking out other potential apartments for rent. I quickly discovered that most people had more money than I did. The only apartment I could afford was the fifty-dollar offer I had received first thing in the morning.

The Mercury Cougar payments I had agreed to in January were now out of the question. I found a car dealer who was willing to trade me straight across for a Volkswagen bug. I may have gotten screwed, but I ended up getting where I needed to go.

The arrangement for the fifty-dollar apartment, which was really a two-story house converted into six small apartments, was completed at 5:00 p.m. that same day. Within two weeks I was attending classes, distributing anti-war leaflets on campus, and banging the girl who lived in the apartment below me.

Everyone who has ever gone through army basic and advanced training knows about Jody. The message about Jody was delivered by a drill instructor with horrible bad breath yelling as loud as he could while his nose was touching yours. If you tried to step back, you would bump into another drill instructor whose chest was up against your back.

As we marched and ran, we would chant rhymes about Jody. The marching cadence count might sound like this;

Ain't no use in goin home, Jody got your gal an gone
Every time you stamp your feet, Jody gets a piece of meat.
Ain't no use in goin back, Jody got your Cadillac
Ain't no use in feelin' blue, Jody got your sister too.

Jody was the mythical stud who was banging your old lady while you were destined to die in some leech-infested shit hole because you were a scumbag, limp dick, faggot maggot who couldn't put one foot in front of the other without fucking it up. The drill instructors made sure everyone hated Jody. Once we were taught to hate Jody, it was easy to hate Charlie or the gooks, slopes, dinks, commies, and fags. Jody was hated and hateful. We were learning.

While taking a bath, I noticed hundreds of little black spots in the water. Later that day a Vietnam veteran biker dude stopped by to smoke a joint and when I told him about the black spots in the bathwater, he said without hesitation, "You got fuckin crabs, man. I had that shit three times in the Nam, man. Your dick's going to fall off, man. You're going to fuckin' die, man. You need to go the college dispensary and get some crab juice, man." I thanked the biker dude for his encouraging remarks and did as he suggested. A few hours later I returned home with a bottle of pink liquid crab repellent.

The next day I spoke to the source of my new experience to give her notice of the problem. During our conversation she suggested the crabs may have come from her husband, whom she had spent one week with in Hawaii. I didn't even know she was married. Apparently he was serving in Vietnam with the US Army, and they had gotten together during his R & R a few weeks before.

As soon as she mentioned Vietnam, my ears perked up. I asked about his job and location in Vietnam, but she knew what most civilians know about the men they send to die in war, which is very little. She did know that he had something to do with mortars. I asked if she had an envelope with his address so I could find out what unit he was in. I stopped breathing briefly when I saw the envelope. It was the same as my old in-theatre address. He was in my unit doing the same job for the same company I had humped with the year before. He brought his wife a two-dollar set of crabs he had purchased from a Vietnamese boom-boom girl, and he generously shared them with her and she in turn shared them with me.

The realization that I had become Jody stung me like an angry wasp. I was banging a chick whose husband was living in a foxhole I may have dug a year earlier. This whole thing freaked me out, and I never again jumped the bones of the crab-factory girl downstairs. She was not lonely for long, and this Jody never got crabs again.

Give Peace a Chance

"There is no contradiction between hating war and
honoring the soldier."

Dr. Jonathan Shay from the book Achilles in Vietnam

B. W. had returned to his home in Fairfax County, Virginia, and
was attending college. He sent me an anti-war leaflet that called
for the American public to show their opposition to the continued
occupation of Vietnam by boycotting all businesses in the United
States for a twenty-four-hour period. I latched on to this idea like
the leeches attached themselves to my balls in the jungles of Vietnam a year earlier. I had leaflets printed at great personal expense.
This was money I didn't have to spare, but the sacrifices and deaths
of my veterans in Vietnam outweighed any personal discomfort. I
was fulfilling a promise to my veterans. They would know I hadn't
forgotten to bring them home if I could.

I knew nothing about trauma-induced behavior at the time. My
actions and beliefs, however, preceded a cognitive awareness of
emotional damage done in Vietnam by more than twenty years.
I had developed a disdain for possessions and bitterness toward
those who whined about the smallest discomfort. I also had a
major problem with authority figures. The experiences in Vietnam had narrowed my personal philosophy to a few basic, short,
emotionally generated sentences that included, "If I can't carry

it on my back, I don't need it," and, more to the point, "If it ain't death, it ain't important." I threw this philosophy in the face of anyone who challenged my perceptions.

There are many negative ramifications to this short, combat-based philosophy. When I say, "If I can't carry it on my back, I don't need it," I am really saying that I don't value possessions. This personal philosophy would prohibit me from owning property or accumulating wealth and other possessions for more than thirty years before I modified the contents.

The second homespun philosophy, "If it ain't death, it ain't important," would cripple my attempts to have intimate relationships and close friendships for the rest of my life. Those who deny the lifelong psychological impact of direct participation in war are, in my opinion, narcissistic blowhards who don't have a clue about the intrinsic nature of humanity. I am convinced that a simple vanity about man's relationship with God lies at the heart of this miscalculation.

The forward observer position I held in Vietnam allowed me to be independent. My home was in my rucksack, and I chose who I traveled with on most days. I approached the anti-war movement with the same tenacity with which I had attacked the vegetation-covered hills in Vietnam. I did not ask permission or seek help in the printing and distribution of the leaflets. Nonetheless, my activities soon caught the attention of other like-minded students on campus.

The first person I hooked up with was a native of Portland. He had medium-length hair, more contemporary than hippie, and a brother who had spent a short time with the marines in Vietnam before he was wounded and sent home. His name was Mike; he was handsome and soft spoken. Mike was a social organizer with an inviting personable demeanor. We lived together for more than three years and had several community-wide successes plus a few failures.

Mike was the magnet and organizer while I was the one who made sure things got done. We started the Ashland people's food co-op by joining seven people who were willing to put two dollars a week into a vegetable fund. At the end of the week, we would take our money to a wholesale food warehouse and buy fourteen dollars worth of fresh vegetables. Our cut of the distributed vegetables was enough to feed Mike and me all week long. As other people joined the group, we began to fill out the papers for a nonprofit corporation status. We sold lifetime memberships for five dollars and within two years opened up a small store using members and volunteers to staff and manage our nonprofit business. The Ashland people's food co-op is still open as of 2012.

Mike became a VISTA volunteer his senior year in college and allowed me to help him with some of his projects. One particular project was to do a drug awareness survey among junior high youth in Jackson County. Mike developed the questionnaire in a professional manner that not only revealed drug use trends but also addressed the youth's perception of the drug's impact on their minds and bodies. We had trick questions in the survey also, which helped us weed out jokesters and bullshitters. We ended up with a gold mine of information Mike would use to address students and administration groups on the subject of teen drug use and perception.

Mike allowed me to help him with a group of troubled youth from a special education class in junior high. Mike's plan was to gather, store, transport, and sell recyclables to distributors and use the money to take the youth on a weekend backpacking trip into the Marble Mountain Wilderness area in Northern California.

Soon after we got started working on the recycling project, the local garbage franchise complained to the city council that we were stealing their business. We had to go to a city council meeting and jump through hoops just to keep going. The garbage disposal franchises in the early '70s were not interested in recycling. They wanted to burn and bury like they had always done. These local-based franchise monopolies fought to maintain the status quo and saw environmental concerns as a threat to their livelihood.

We continued to collect and store recyclables throughout the winter and spring months. Our next problem centered on how to transport the material to a plant willing and capable of processing it. I put on my best military smile and approached the local National Guard who had two-and-a-half-ton trucks in their motor pool. The guard quickly agreed to help and considered their contribution good public relations. The military was in need of an improved image as the anti–Vietnam War protests continued to put pressure on the social and economic foundations of the nation.

The money we made off the recycling project was nowhere near enough to cover the costs of the planned backpacking trip into the California wilderness. I think Mike filled in the gaps by soliciting donations from the local community. The original plan to teach the youth how to trust adults and work together toward a common goal had been a success. The backpacking trip was their reward for a job well done, but it also served to remind me once again how far I was from returning from Vietnam.

The hike from the trailhead to the lake we planned to set up camp on was perhaps five miles. Not long after leaving the van, we encountered a very large rattlesnake sunning itself across our path. The snake posed no real threat, but that few seconds of potential danger, the scared looks on the faces of the students, the backpacks we carried, and the column of people brought on a flashback that I would address the same way I responded to the ever-present and demanding awareness of Vietnam. I put my head down, took possession of the point, and charged forward so I would be the first to encounter any new or unexpected challenge. I outran the column by never stopping to catch my wind or take a drink of water. When I reached the high mountain lake, I had a terrible headache and was way past dehydration. I was too old at twenty-five to walk through heat exhaustion again, but I had done it anyway. I knew what I was doing, but I did it anyway. My reaction was compulsive.

I was still unaware of what a flashback or intrusive mental thought or PTSD was. It awoke like a roaring lion inside of me and, without my knowledge or awareness, urged me to continue a pursuit of substance abuse and self-destructive behavior.

Once again the social activist Mike recruited my help to organize a crisis phone center and recruited the band of long hairs from Southern Oregon College to man the phones. This direct non-punitive and confidential one-on-one approach to emerging crisis was very effective. We responded to, among other things, teen suicide, unwanted pregnancies, wanted pregnancies, and drug overdose. I did well with suicide and drug overdose but dropped the ball on the intricacies of pregnancies. Thank God for Planned Parenthood because without them I wouldn't have known what to do.

Early my first year of school I hooked up with Tom, who was a native of New York and a very social creature. Mike and I became instrumental in getting Tom elected as student body president a few years later. Tom attended law school and eventually became a successful attorney.

In January 2012, as I worked on the completion this book, I received word that my marine veteran friend Al had committed suicide while sitting in his pickup near a lake in Western Oregon. Al ate a bullet approximately twenty-five years after returning home from Vietnam. His best friend said the demons of war visited Al most nights. I do not believe he ever went to the Veterans Administration for help. He shared his greatest war-related traumas with very few. I will miss him.

During the late '60s, Al was the third and possibly best connection I made during these early college days partly because of his military background. Al was a Vietnam combat marine veteran who was missing two fingers on his left hand as a result of a grenade explosion. He boasted a body count in the mid-teens including one unarmed female. Body count means a lot to marines and the number Al claimed earned him respect in the insanely macho marine community.

Some of the anti-war missions Al and I planned were amusingly dangerous. Some of the plans we followed through on were off the wall and in your face. I will get to those later. Al did not look like a hippie. His clothes were off-the-shelf Sears and Roebuck, and he chain-smoked Marlboros. We were both obsessed with the board game Risk and played it relentlessly.

Al took the lead in organizing the NORML (National Organization for the Reform of Marijuana Laws) project. We delivered our box of signatures to the secretary of state's office and helped to put the measure on the ballot that election cycle. The measure failed in the general election, but it wasn't because we didn't try.

Within weeks of my moving into the fifty-dollar-per-month apartment, Mike began having money problems, so I insisted he move in with me. We lived, worked, and played together for several years planning and organizing anti-war and socially conscious activities. The thing that made us a good team was Mike's charming, engaging demeanor and my radical, in-your-face, kill-them-all-and-let-God-sort-them-out combat-generated anger.

I quickly established a pattern dictated by the amount of money I would receive from the GI Bill. On the first day of each term, I would take out a short-term loan from the school and use it to pay tuition. Each month when I received the check from the Veterans Administration, I would pay off one-third of the short-term loan. At the end of the term, I would have paid back the school loan and I would repeat the process. The GI Bill allowed me to pursue higher education, but it did not pay the bills. After tuition, books, rent, and utilities, I was left with twenty dollars a month for food. The low-income status I had achieved through much effort qualified me for food stamps and other poverty-related programs sponsored by various government agencies. I lived mostly on potatoes. You can buy a lot of potatoes with twenty dollars. I had so much starch in my body that I walked straight legged.

I settled into the daily class routine as my hair grew longer than a wooly mammoth's. The off-the-shelf clothes from high school still fit me, so I wore them until they were beyond repair. I purchased replacement attire at a Salvation Army store in Medford, Oregon. It took very little time for me to transition from a neatly dressed physically fit twenty-one-year-old combat veteran to an angry, muscle-bound, long-haired hippie with an attitude and a full beard dressed in ill-fitting Salvation Army garb that made me look like I was between fixes. I was perfecting the art of withdrawal from society by making myself unattractive. I didn't know this at the time, but the evidence would linger until I slipped it in the proper slot more than thirty years later. I thought I was slapping America in the face in an act of open bitter resentment at my experiences in Vietnam. Life is full of these great lessons.

The class schedule I adopted was as unorthodox and antiestablishment as my choice of dress. I never believed in homework while in high school. I believed in sports, grab-ass, and spitball but not homework. I practiced being a class clown and a smart-ass but not how to study. But now, after surviving war, I couldn't read enough about Asia, China, Russia, Communism, Buddhism, and Socialism. I had been taught that America was the greatest country in the world, but my experiences in Vietnam said we were morally no better than anyone else. I sought firm answers because I was confused and pissed.

I skipped over English 101, Math 101, and the other standard first-year classes. I concluded that these classes were for kids straight out of high school who had innocent dreams of getting a degree and becoming successful in society. I wanted to end the war and punish the ones who were killing my veterans. By the end of my second term, I was taking classes with titles such as Environmentalism, Nonviolent Revolution, Utopian Societies, Advanced Poetry, and Creative Writing. Every one of these classes was at the 400 honors level. I was surprised to find that this desire to learn came out of me; after all, I had graduated high school with a 1.4 GPA. I also studied Buddhism and took several classes in law enforcement because one of my brothers was a career law enforcement officer, and I hoped that taking classes on the subject would help us understand each other.

The driving question in my mind was this: "If America is the greatest nation in the world, why did we invade a country that posed no threat to us, and, more important, how come Americans were engaged in the murder, rape, and mutilation of unarmed civilians?" I concluded that I could answer my own questions if I studied the two leading Communist powers at the time, which happened to be China and Russia. I looked to the Communist systems that we were compared to so I might discover the reasons behind our greatness.

The study of Russian history allowed me to see a people who were the embodiment of the Russian Bear, which is their national symbol. I studied Russian history to learn the executive and judicial systems. I found a people who were deeply orthodox Catholics at their base. Less than 10 percent of the population was Communist, and this loyalty was rewarded with powerful positions within the system.

The defense of Stalingrad against the German assault during WWII resulted in one million casualties and produced Russian heroes both male and female. A female sniper killed more than six hundred Germans to set a record.

I read the autobiography of Marshal Zhukov, who was one of the great generals to come out of WWII. His success at defeating the Germans would worry the power elite in Moscow, who would see fit to force Zhukov to choose between death by firing squad and suicide by his own hand. He ate a bullet.

The following is a brief overview of some of the players and the ideological elements they studied. Karl Heinrich Marx is first on the list. He was a German philosopher, political economist, historian, and political theorist, sociologist, and revolutionary socialist who developed the sociopolitical theory of Marxism. His Marxist ideas played a significant role in the development of modern social science and also in the socialist political movement. He published various books during his lifetime, with the most notable being *The Communist Manifesto* and *Capital* , many of which were co-written with his friend, the fellow German revolutionary socialist Friedrich Engels.

Marx's widespread influence revolves around his ethical message: a "morally empowering language of critique" against the dominant capitalist society. Marx predicted that capitalism, like previous socioeconomic systems, would inevitably produce internal tensions, which would lead to its self-destruction and replacement by a new system. Just as capitalism replaced feudalism, he believed socialism would, in its turn, replace capitalism, and lead to a stateless, classless society called pure Communism. This would emerge after a transitional period called the "dictatorship of the proletariat," a period sometimes referred to as the "worker's state" or "worker's democracy." Marx also argued that socioeconomic change occurred through organized revolutionary action and that both social theorists and underprivileged people should act to carry it out.

The Communist Manifesto was nothing like I had been told. The final phase was a society that existed without government control. In a society of this type, every citizen knew and understood the rules thus eliminating the need for a governing body.

This sounds utopian, but in my study of utopian societies, it became clear that all forms of government are utopian for at least some of the people in the state. The rich and powerful will sing the praises of whatever society has elevated them to a position of authority while the majority of the downtrodden plot their overthrow.

Twentieth century China accepted the Marxist theory of communism after it had undergone many Mao Zedong sponsored revisions. Communism in China became, "Maoism". It is difficult to recognize Maoism in today's China although the Maoest party has active groups in Peru, India and Napal.

During the study of China's history, I was most impressed with the story and legend of the Long March during WWII. I personally consider the Long March to be one of the greatest military achievements in history. The Long March makes William Tecumseh Sherman's march to the sea look like a Sunday picnic. Sherman traveled three hundred miles in five weeks and returned with

90 percent of his army, whereas the Long March covered eight thousand miles in twelve months and ended the campaign with less than 10 percent of the number they started with. Both campaigns have been studied worldwide, and many serious notes have been taken by military experts.

Mao was a politician and a poet, whereas Zhou Enlai was a military tactician. They fought to defeat the Japanese at the same time they struggled to rid China of the allied-backed shadow government of Chiang Kai-shek. Chiang Kai-shek would be defeated by Mao in China and forced to flee to Taiwan with the Kuomintang and, some say, eighteen trainloads of priceless antiques from throughout China. I have heard stories about the Kuomintang reaching out from Taiwan and stealing raw opium from the mountain peoples of Laos and Vietnam. They would sometimes transport this opium on Air America flights to distribution points in America and Europe. Air America was a front company for the CIA in Asia.

Eventually Mao would fall prey to the paranoia that grips all dictators. He would kill or imprison all who opposed him in his mind. His policies of land redistribution and social reform would fail terribly and leave China to suffer for generations. He was a great leader until he decided to consolidate and retain the power he had achieved by killing all his friends.

The conclusion of my nation study was that America was not the best nation in the world, but neither was any other nation. Every type of ruling system was dominated by the few. True democracy existed nowhere.

"Sex, drugs, and rock and roll" was the mantra of the counter-culture in America during the late '60s. This mantra was a clever contemporary quote, but it also was a diversion from the task of confronting the military industrial complex that was making billions of dollars by killing my veterans in some leech-infested shit hole. The war in Vietnam was not serving the American public. The North Vietnamese possessed neither the will nor the means to attack America on our home soil. The people who thanked us veterans for defending our country were delusional. We had invaded another country, not defended our own.

Vietnam was being supported at home by American citizens who believed that we had the right to invade anyone we wanted. I was convinced that the war supporters were obsessed with winning without regard for what was right or wrong. The domino theory and the contrived Gulf of Tonkin incident relating to Vietnam were not much different than the lies about weapons of mass destruction that preceded the invasion of Iraq more than forty years later.

Two separate occurrences stand out as events that served to convince me that Vietnam was the wrong war, at the wrong time, and in the wrong place. The first example took place while I was in the field. The point element engaged one military-age male packing a weapon. They shot the VC (Vietnamese Communist) in the back eight times as he ran away. The VC went into the hooch and then left the hooch to seek cover in a spider hole. The grunts followed the blood trail left behind by the VC. They threw a grenade in the hole and attempted to pull the VC out only to discover that he was still alive. The grunts threw another grenade in the hole and then pulled the wounded VC out into the open. The VC lived for an additional ten minutes before he died. I followed all of this action on the radio.

This is the way I would fight if anyone ever attacked Oregon. I would fight to the death, and death would not come easily, because Oregon was my home and I had no other place to go. That's what the VC with eight M16 holes and two grenades in his body was doing. He was fighting to the last breath, and death would not come easily, because Vietnam was his home and he had nowhere else to go.

The second incident that helped to convince me that Vietnam was the wrong war, at the wrong time, and in the wrong place happened after I came out of the field. I was talking to an old Vietnamese woman who washed my clothes and sold me weed on a regular basis. One day I asked her what she thought about the North Vietnamese leader, Ho Chi Minh.

She said to me, "Ho Chi Minh same-same you George Washington."

In other words, she said that Ho Chi Minh was the father of Vietnam the same way George Washington was the father of the United States. The declaration of this Vietnamese laundry lady upset my preconceived notions about America's true purpose in Vietnam. I would not know the full story until I read the complete history of Vietnam more than twenty years later.

The history of Vietnam shows us a land that has been seeking independence from all outside influences for thousands of years. If the Vietnamese were Communists in the 1960s, it was because the allied powers had rejected their peace offerings, which forced the Vietnamese to seek weapons and supplies from behind the iron curtain in Communist-controlled China and Russia.

The Vietnamese first appeared in history as one of many scattered peoples living in what is now South China and Northern Vietnam just before the beginning of the Christian era. According to local tradition, the small Vietnamese kingdom of Au Lac, located in the heart of the Red River valley, was founded by a line of legendary kings who had ruled over the ancient kingdom of Van Lang for thousands of years. Historical evidence to substantiate this tradition is scanty.

In 111 BC, Chinese armies conquered Nam Viet and absorbed it into the growing Han Empire. The Chinese conquest had fateful consequences for the future course of Vietnamese history. The most famous early revolt took place in AD 39, when two widows of local aristocrats, the Trung sisters, led an uprising against foreign rule. The revolt was briefly successful, and the older sister, Trung Trac, established herself as ruler of an independent state. The Chinese armies returned to the attack, and in AD 43 Vietnam was conquered again.

Finally, in 939, Vietnamese forces under Ngo Quyen took advantage of chaotic conditions in China to defeat local occupation troops and set up an independent state.

Confucianism continued to provide the foundation for the political institutions of the state. Everything reflected the Chinese model. At the village level, social mores reflected native forms more than patterns imported from China. Although to the superficial eye Vietnam looked like a "smaller dragon," under the tutelage of the great empire to the north, it continued to have a separate culture with vibrant traditions of its own.

Vietnam has pursued independence for thousands of years. It was the first nation in the world to grant women the right to own property. It made friendship overtures to President Abraham Lincoln, and at one point Old Ironsides dropped anchor in the Gulf of Tonkin. After WWII the Viet peoples sought a peace treaty with the United States, but it was rejected by the postwar administration.

The French had established a colonial occupation of Vietnam before WWII. They considered it their rite of passage to colonize the poor ignorant Vietnamese and levy excessive fees and abusive rule over the natives. The French were defeated at home in less than a month at the onset of WWII, but they maintained a foothold in Vietnam and at one time shared colonial rule with the

Japanese over Vietnam. At the time Vietnam was created by combining Cochinchina with southern Annam.

The French were defeated at the battle of Dien Bien Phu in March 1954. In Geneva that same year, an accord established the 17th parallel as a demarcation line thus creating two Vietnams, north and south. In 1955 the American-backed president of South Vietnam refused to hold scheduled elections and later declared himself president of South Vietnam. Soon after Diem took control of government, a massive redistribution of land resulted in Diem's supporters taking control of large sections of South Vietnam.

The United States had spent billions of dollars to support the French colonial policies in Asia. The French people were tired of war and did not support the military's colonial involvement in Southeast Asia after WWII.

The Americans would then embark on a different course of action that would put US ground troops in direct combat with the North Vietnamese Army, resulting in more than fifty-eight thousand US deaths. Statistics would reveal that more than sixty-three thousand Vietnam veterans would commit suicide after returning home. The suicide rate of returning veterans from the desert wars in Iraq and Afghanistan would eclipse the Vietnam figures. Something is terribly wrong here.

In 1971 I was a volunteer worker for the campaign to elect Wayne Morse to the US Senate. Wayne Morse was one of only two senators to vote against the Gulf of Tonkin Resolution. I took part in organizing a campus appearance for Mr. Morse, and, after a hard day of making speeches and answering questions, he and a small group of supporters gathered in an upstairs meeting room above the student union to consume coffee, cookies, and bullshit. That evening Wayne Morse told us two things that I will share with you.

First, Mr. Morse told us that the Gulf of Tonkin Resolution was drafted one month before the incident that carries its name. Mr. Morse went on to say that the Gulf of Tonkin incident was a contrived event. The nonincident was used to pass the resolution, and the resolution was used to rush to war. Sort of like the weapons of mass destruction used to lead Americans into invading Iraq, and the contrived incident the Germans fostered to start military conflict at the beginning of WWII with Poland.

Later that evening, Wayne Morse told us that he was standing in a room having drinks with President Kennedy when Kennedy announced that he had been led to the wrong conclusions by his intelligence advisors. President Kennedy said that as a result, he had decided to remove all military advisors from South Vietnam. President Kennedy added that he would not deploy ground forces to Southeast Asia. Two weeks after making this statement, President Kennedy was assassinated in Texas.

Ashland, Oregon, is home to a fine arts community anchored by the internationally famous and world-class Oregon Shakespeare Festival. The town of approximately twenty thousand people is situated on the southern tip of the Rogue Valley. The gentle climate and natural inversion of the valley facilitates the commercial growth of fruit, and the campus of Southern Oregon College contributes to the academic appeal of the community.

The anti-war activities we pursued in the Rogue Valley rattled the cages of college administrators, police, and many citizens of this peaceful community. In other words, we were moderately successful at introducing the true cost of the war in terms of lives lost and anger developed. We also attempted to introduce doubt and fear into the political minds of conservative Americans who before our existence could support wars—notice I didn't say "go to war themselves"—without feeling the truth of their actions.

At some point during our anti-war activities, Al, the combat marine veteran, and I conjured up a ridiculous plan to educate local citizens by bringing the war home to the masses. We felt that some war supporters were hiding behind closed doors and pretending that teenage American boys were not dying in Asia. Al and I wanted to remind them in a way they wouldn't forget.

We began developing plans to build a mortar capable of delivering nonlethal paint bomb ordinance onto the village of Ashland. Our target village was bordered on two sides by the foothills of the Siskiyou mountain range. Mortars can be effectively used if given an elevation advantage over the target area. The high-angle indirect fire capabilities of the mortar would allow us to lob ordinance onto the target. All other forms of artillery have a lower trajectory, and the artillery pieces are difficult to break down and reposition.

Our next problem involved building containers that were strong enough to withstand the shock of being launched into the air but would not be lethal to living things on impact. We decided to build rounds that would explode in the air before reaching the ground. The ordinance inside the airburst rounds would be blood red paint with leaflets protected inside balloons advising the village occupants that they were in a free- fire zone and must leave the area or suffer the consequences.

The plan had more than a few flaws, but that didn't stop us from hashing it over for hours while taking turns on the Risk board game. We eventually concluded that the mortar-and-paint plan would be put on the back burner until further notice.

The leaflets originally planned for the mortar attack would be delivered in other, more conventional ways. Al had left two fingers behind in Vietnam and had thrown his Purple Heart and other medals onto the White House lawn in protest of the war. He had, however, brought home the official-sounding vocabulary necessary to reproduce military-style documents using all the proper acronyms and jargon. We developed, printed, and distributed hundreds of these leaflets throughout the Ashland village.

The official-looking leaflets Al wrote basically told the citizens of Ashland that the entire area had been declared a free-fire zone. It informed the villagers that they had twenty-four hours to relocate. If they chose to remain in the free-fire zone after the deadline, they would be considered enemy combatants and we would not be responsible for the consequences.

As I was delivering flyers house to house in the neighborhood close to my apartment, which was across the street from Lithia Park and the police station, it occurred to me that I should check in with the police to make sure our leaflet distribution was within the law. The police were happy to see me.

I showed them one of the leaflets and asked if I was breaking any laws. They informed me that my actions were within the law as long as I didn't put the leaflets inside mailboxes. They also said that its dispatch had received dozens of phone calls from frightened senior citizens who were upset and confused by the contents of the flyers. Al and I took this as a sign that our mission was a success.

The score was one to one. Our mortar plan didn't work out, but the leaflets did. We had engaged the enemy, and they were off-balance. While they responded with confusion and fear, we were running deep reconnaissance missions.

Al looked like one of them. His hair was short, and he was clean-shaven. His dress was conservative, and his speech was proper and respectful. He was a registered Republican and a member of several politically right groups including the John Birch Society. He knew more about the enemy than they did about him. He was a mole and a wealth of information.

Somewhere along the line of our protests, we planned, organized, and executed a guerrilla theater on campus. Some of the anti-war regulars dressed up like Vietnamese civilians and set up a mock village on the campus lawn. Al and I dressed in military clothes complete with plastic M16s, jungle knives, and fake grenades. We filled the grenades with red dye and salt. The red dye could be simulated blood or napalm in my mind, and the salt would leave a permanent stain of dead grass on the campus lawn as a reminder of the war in Vietnam.

The Vietnamese civilian actors set up camp on the lawn and pretended to farm, eat, and work. About twenty minutes later, Al and I showed up and started "killing" any Vietnamese who tried to run. We captured the people we didn't kill, cut them up with our knives, and beat them until they stayed down. Our acting was less than convincing, but we achieved our goal of keeping the war in their face. We couldn't forget about Vietnam, and we wouldn't let them forget either.

When school let out for summer break, I always found a job to support myself. The jobs ranged from logging in Eastern Oregon to working as a salesman for Radio Shack. I also worked concrete for a contractor and drove an eighteen-wheeler cross-country. Summer employment provided me with the opportunity to earn a little money and take a break from the demands of the anti-war movement. The money was critical as the GI Bill did not come close to covering the costs associated with higher education. My parents had raised six children on low wages, and I was reluctant to ask them for money unless it was a loan with a payback schedule.

After I had grown hair for a year, I started looking for summer work. I soon got a job with a logging company in Southern Washington. I was a long-haired hippie running a chain saw to bump knots on a landing where they would collect logs for loading onto trucks. This was redneck country, where all long-haired hippies were commie fags. The second day on the job, one of the two owners started suggesting that he and the crew take me down and cut my hair. It didn't take me long to get in the face of the boss and let him know that if he touched me he might as well kill me, because if he didn't I would rape his wife, burn his house, destroy all his logging equipment, and kill everyone in his fucking family. I told him that I would destroy everything in his life and then I would come after him, just like the gooks taught me in Vietnam.

By the end of the first week on the job, that same boss couldn't stop talking about how good of a worker I was. He never again mentioned cutting my hair. The irony is that the boss who threatened me was a full-blown alcoholic who would show up for work drunk and sometimes get in a fistfight with his brother in the middle of the landing.

The best summer job I ever had was a 181-mile trail maintenance contract on the Pacific Crest National Scenic Trail in Southern Oregon. The trails in the contract were in a wilderness area along the crest of the Cascade mountain range.

I borrowed enough money from my parents to purchase tools, dehydrated foods, and backpacks. I also bought two sleeping bags, canteens, and a backpacking camp stove. At the end of the contract, I repaid every penny my parents had loaned me. I had brothers and sisters who had borrowed money from my parents and never paid it back. That would be like becoming Jody again for me, and I had no intention of going there.

Extensive planning is required to take on a project of this size. I collected detailed maps of the area and planned out each week's worth of work. Al and I would set up a strategically located spike camp and work all the trails in that area. On Saturday morning the second team would pack a week's worth of food and supplies into a prearranged location. The team would then work a section of trail on the way back to their vehicles and return to town for the week.

Al and I would rendezvous with the supplies and either relocate the food stash or set up a new camp and work the trails in that area until we could repeat the process the next week. We went four weeks without a bath. Both of us had gone more than four weeks between baths in Vietnam, but that experience didn't make it any easier to live with our own smells.

I need to say here that my college friendships with Al, Mike, Tom, and the mother of my children would fade away over time. My relationships with military friends and biological family members would also turn cold. I would destroy most relationships on a regular basis as a direct result of the PTSD I brought home from Vietnam. I didn't know about PTSD at the time, but I was headed in a direction that would transform me into a freaking expert on the subject before I turned sixty. I didn't choose any of this, but it would turn out that way without asking my permission. I claim a constant relationship with hypervigilance and severe noise and light discipline in my area of influence. I am not attracted to crowds. I am not sure I chose these behaviors, but I have learned to manage them.

The bulk of the trail maintenance work was done by me and my conservative radical friend, Al. We were two Vietnam veteran grunts packing heavy loads in difficult terrain and living close to the ground. We stayed in the mountains for thirty days in a row on the project. We had some hard times with blisters and sore feet, but the experience packed its own weight and gave us great stories to tell.

The trail maintenance contract included two special projects. The first special project involved removing a section of a three-foot-diameter pine tree that had fallen across a trail. The contract was in a wilderness area that prohibited the use of any gas-operated power equipment. This meant we had to use hand tools to remove the log from the trail.

I was always willing to take on the most difficult projects myself. On the day of the scheduled removal of the pine tree, both teams came together. The town-based team had located a hand-operated crosscut saw, also known as a misery whip. The saw was called a misery whip for a reason. The town-based trail maintenance team planned to arrive at the trailhead by 10:00 a.m., hike to the project site, and remove the log section in the afternoon.

At seven in the morning, I left Al at the trailhead to hook up with the second team while I hiked into the project to see if I could chop the log in half with a double-bladed ax. If you think of Paul Bunyan, you will have the right picture. In order to clear the trail, we would need to cut completely through the log two times before rolling the centerpiece off the trail. I attacked the first cut with my ax. Two hours later both hands had the three Bs: bleeding, busted, blisters. The first cut was only three quarters complete, but my hands were 100 percent done.

The second team arrived, and we took turns strapping ourselves to one of the ends of the misery whip. None of us had used a crosscut saw before, but mistakes are the foundation of all new knowledge. We fought the misery whip until it wore us out. Once fatigued and searching for an easier way to complete the task, we fell into the natural rhythm of the crosscut saw. We had been cutting straight back and forth with little success. After succumbing to fatigue, we began to rock the saw like a gentle swing—low on one end and high on the other.

Less than an hour after capturing the rhythm of the saw, our project was complete. The Paul Bunyan imitation left me with two bleeding hands and a new respect for the misery whip.

The second separate bid item on the contract called for us to reposition a footbridge that had been washed downstream during a spring flash flood. I started preparing for this project the first time the contracting officer from the US Forest Service came into the woods to inspect our work. This forest service employee was riding a horse, but what impressed me was the mule he led that packed his camping equipment. I had never seen a mule so big and strong. I instantly started praising his fine mule and joking that he needed to bring it on the day we moved the footbridge. We got along well with the contracting officer. He liked the idea of two Vietnam veterans living in the wilderness, and I liked his mule.

On the day of the footbridge project, we rounded up all the long-haired hippie war protesters we could find who were willing to lend a hand. We were able to reposition the bridge using brute strength five minutes before the forest contract officer arrived with his big beautiful mule. The footbridge completed my contractual obligations to the US Forest Service. We passed final inspection and received full payment for the contract without penalty.

A group of us who had worked on the trail maintenance contract made one last trip into the wilderness to enjoy the scenery and visit a special place we had found. While working on the trail, we didn't have time to let the beauty and majestic qualities of the Pacific Crest National Scenic Trail amaze us as it should. We had no need for backpacks and tools, so we dressed in cutoffs and tennis shoes. Our destination was a waterfall approximately eighty feet high. The water was so cold that as soon as we jumped in, we had to fight to come to the surface and return to shore. Everyone jumped in once but not twice. Very few people had seen, let alone jumped into, this waterfall-fed pond. It was our secret.

One of the classes I took in college was called Nonviolent Revolution. The second week of class the instructor presented us with a hypothetical situation that involved a family consisting of four people who were walking down the sidewalk after dark. In the situation, the family is confronted by an armed criminal who threatens to kill the father and rape the female family members at gunpoint. The professor asked the class what they would do in this situation. The class struggled to come up with nonviolent solutions to the problem.

Eventually it became my turn to respond to the problem. I told the class that I had been in a similar situation in Vietnam and, although the people in Asia were not my family, I could never allow rape to happen on my watch again. I assured them that I would do anything to attack, disarm, and, if need be, kill the assailant. That one lesson convinced me that I was not a person who believed in a nonviolent response to a violent situation. I had learned what I needed to know from that class and soon after dropped it from my schedule.

A class in early Japanese court poetry opened the door to a deeper study of Asian religion and history. I bargained with the instructor on course requirements until she allowed me to complete all course requirements except the final term paper. In place of the standard paper, I was allowed to produce an analysis and comparison between Eastern and Western religions. I read everything I could get my hands on concerning Buddhism. I reasoned that knowing a people's religion allows us to see their heart.

The Clergy and Laity Concerned (CLC) about the war in Vietnam was a faith-based organization that had become disillusioned with the war. Its members no longer believed the propaganda about the domino theory, and they were uncertain about the truth of the Gulf of Tonkin incident. The nice thing about these folks, in my opinion, was that they carried a big stick.

Tom, who was by then the student body president, was contacted by a local anti-war senior citizen who belonged to the clergy group. She offered Tom an all-expense-paid trip to a CLC conference in Boulder, Colorado. Tom accepted the offer and indicated that he wanted to take me along because of my knowledge of the war and the military.

As we descended from our cruising level over Boulder, Colorado, the passenger jet hit an air pocket. I estimated that we dropped about a thousand feet in the next two seconds. The magazine I was reading ended up in the hands of the person next to me. The person in front of me ended up in the lap of the person next to them, and everything in the overhead compartment was set free to fly wherever it wanted to. This was not the first time I had encountered a short thrill on an airplane preparing to land. I was reminded of the C-130 on approach with a smoking electrical panel just outside Cam Ranh Bay and the Chinook helicopter that had hit an air pocket and dropped several hundred feet while lifting us out of some scary jungle country north of our usual AO (area of operation) in South Vietnam. I am not a great fan of flying, and perhaps the burning plane and the roller-coaster air-pocket thrills were sending me a message.

The CLC was composed of religious, rational people determined to put pressure on the corporations to end the war. Their plan was simple and, I am certain, effective. They intended to identify the corporations that produced the weapons and equipment that allowed the war in Asia to continue. They would then gather tens of thousands of proxy votes and demand that the targeted company stop producing the tools of war. The CLC had the stocks to back up their demands. The companies would have no choice. My role was to help the CLC identify the evil products of war such as napalm, defoliants, and Bouncing Betties. Some of the corporations we identified were Westinghouse, DuPont, Dow Chemical, General Electric, and Bell Helicopter.

The information I provided was more important to the CLC than the fact that I still had one foot and all of my mouth in Vietnam. At a communal dinner, I would burst out in grunt speak with lines like; "Pass the fucking potatoes." They loved me for my crude honesty, and, even though I embarrassed myself frequently, I respected the hell out of them. They were going to bring my veterans home.

I had a lengthy conversation with a female who had returned from Vietnam just weeks before the CLC conference. She was a contract employee of the United Nations and had been dispatched to Vietnam to gauge the amount of theft and/or profiteering occurring on the docks where American ships unloaded their cargo.

She told of meeting a young Vietnamese male who boasted that he could get anything he wanted off the docks. She was skeptical about his claims but decided to play along. She told the Vietnamese to get her a tractor before she had to leave the country in one week. The Vietnamese male said, "No problem. You come back tomorrow at same place, at same time."

She arrived at the meeting place at the scheduled hour and was taken into a large covered building similar to a basketball court. In the middle of the floor sat a brand-new John Deere tractor.

The Vietnamese male asked, "You want more?"

The United Nations employee told me that her research indicated that as much as 50 percent of all off-loaded equipment and supplies were stolen right off the docks. America was basically supplying arms and equipment to both sides in this war. The corporations were making twice as much profit and my veterans were dying.

On April 30, 1970, American and South Vietnamese forces attacked Communist sanctuaries in Cambodia. On May 4 the Ohio

National Guard opened fire on unarmed Kent State students, some of which were not involved in the anti-war protests. The frightened and poorly led guardsmen fired sixty-seven rounds over a thirteen-second period resulting in four dead and nine wounded Kent State students. The national mood about Vietnam would continue to sour in light of this event.

After receiving word of the Kent State murders, the organizers of the Southern Oregon anti-war movement held an all-night meeting. The time was spent printing leaflets and planning a candlelight parade followed by an all-night vigil for the dead and wounded at Kent State.

At a student rally the next day, an argument broke out between those on the left wanting to lower the flag to half-mast in honor of the victims at Kent State and those on the right who wanted the flag to stay where it was because they liked killing unarmed American kids. When the debate was nearing a shouting match, I left the building and pulled a recon on the flagpole in question. The ruling of the college administration was that the flag would stay at its highest point. At a private meeting of campus anti-war organizers later that night, I told them of my recon mission of the flagpole. I suggested that we remove the flagpole altogether thus denying the war lovers the sense of victory the administration ruling had offered. The flagpole was attached to the support with two bolts. If we removed the bolts, the pole would fall over and we could steal it away. I am not sure where we would have hidden the pole. It is not like we could hide a forty-foot flagpole in a bedroom. I was overruled.

The planned candlelight parade and all-night vigil drew the attention of pro-war conservatives. Our anti-war spokesmen, Mike and Tom, were contacted by local members of the National Rifle Association and the John Birch Society, who requested a face-to-face meeting at the student union. Mike and Tom asked me to join them at the meeting and I agreed.

It was not a big surprise to learn that right-leaning groups had a foothold in Southern Oregon. At one time the national headquarters of the KKK was located in Grants Pass, Oregon, approximately fifty miles north of Ashland along Interstate 5. Longshoremen attempts to unionize in Portland were met with violent armed Pinkerton attacks resulting in nineteen dead on the Oregon docks. Oregon was one of the last states in the union to abolish the "sundowner laws" that imposed a dusk-to-dawn curfew on people of color. Racism and anticollective bargaining sentiment have had a long history in Oregon, but it should be noted that racial equality and unionized workplaces have enjoyed success in the state as well.

The meeting bounced along awkwardly until one of the conservative pro-war supporters issued a veiled threat that implied that people could get hurt if we didn't cancel the scheduled peace march. We had acquired all the legal permits to hold a candlelight march and vigil, but these bullies wanted to take the law into their own hands.

My face went combat crazy on these two pro-war monsters. I jumped up from my chair and leaned over the table in an intimidating fashion. My teeth were clinched and my muscles were spring-fucking tight. In less than one minute I let them know that I didn't remember seeing their limp dicks in my foxhole while in Vietnam. I suggested that if they fucked with me they should bring along a lunch and a friend. The lunch because it was going to take them a little longer than they thought, and the friend because they might need some help getting home. The people on the other side of the table were expecting to meet some pinky, commie, fag, hippie with flowers in his hair. They had no idea that the person at the table with the longest hair was an angry combat veteran who knew how to handle weapons or set an ambush and blow things up. The meeting ended without consensus soon after I exploded. I had not learned to play well with strangers.

After the encounter I organized and trained a group of emergency responders who would act as medics during the candlelight vigil. We filled backpacks with bandages made of torn-up sheets. I showed them how to make a tourniquet out of a belt and how to apply direct pressure to a wound. I showed them how to use plastic to seal a sucking chest wound and instructed them to find the exit hole, because that is where the greatest damage would be. We put red crosses on shirts and bags to help identify the medic teams. This was done only to instill confidence in the medics. I didn't think the crosses would make any difference. If they would kill unarmed students in Kent State, they would shoot red crosses in Ashland. I also helped to instruct outriders who would march alongside the parade and act as early warning, listening, and observation posts. My military training would be used to encourage and organize for peace.

The parade and all-night vigil went on as planned. I did, however, spot the John Birches cruising by the candlelight march in a pickup. I recognized one of the bullies in the passenger seat of a slow-moving rig. When we made eye contact, he flashed a handgun for me. I had seen weapons before. I did not fail to register the threat, and, after the vehicle was out of sight, I quietly passed the word to the other outriders suggesting we direct the parade participants into the trees to the east of the sidewalk if I gave them a signal.

The face-to-face bully tactics didn't work for those who threatened the freedom of speech, but that didn't mean they gave up. They were armed, and the Americans they hated were not. Bullies love this kind of a situation. That's why they are called bullies.

The one thing that amazes me to this day is why the John Birch supporters are willing to kill their own citizens in order to wipe away opposition to their concept of the world. I am forced to ask the obvious question: "What are they afraid of?"

The prospect of violence from armed bullies forced me to re-evaluate my relationship with the anti-war movement. My commitment was to bring all veterans home, and nothing could divert me from that cause. The fact that I still smoked weed and occasionally dropped a passing hit of this and that could pose a problem. If I were to get busted for drugs, it could hurt my anti-war efforts. I would hate to think that another grunt died just because I smoked a joint. I had to make a choice between my veterans and smoke. My veterans won; I knew they would.

Someone gave me a paper called "Post Combat Stress" in the early '70s. This was the first time I had seen anything addressing the possible traumatic consequences of taking part in the Vietnam War. I was highly critical of this paper at the time. I felt it didn't go far enough. Later I would come to understand that this paper was only the opening salvo in a barrage of information that would result in the clinical designation of post-traumatic stress disorder (PTSD) as a recognized psychological condition.

I began to have isolated dreams and flashbacks about Vietnam. I didn't understand what was happening, and I certainly couldn't put anything into words. I began self-medicating with alcohol, which led to problems with abuse and PTSD and all relationships with everybody, everywhere.

On a hot summer day in late August of an unknown year, Mike and I drove into the Ashland foothills to swim in a cold mountain spring. Something snapped while we were at the water. My attitude changed to hyperalert, and I realized a foreboding wave washing over my existence. I was on the edge of something I didn't understand, and I felt like I needed an M16 in my hands.

I asked Mike if he could finish his swim so we could go back to town. Mike took the lead as we walked out of the woods. After traveling down the trail for a hundred yards, I realized that I had opened the gap between us so that if either of us hit a mine, the other would be safe from the blast. I dropped to my knees and began crying. I couldn't understand how Vietnam had gotten into the Siskiyou National Forest. I drank more booze that night.

I began writing poetry to a high school girlfriend during the cold winter months. On spring break I hitchhiked to Montana, and we drove her car back to Ashland. We ended up staying together for eight years and had two boys. All of these relationships would fade away over time. My high school and Vietnam relationships would also end eventually, suddenly or over time. It would take longer to chase my family away, but I would be successful at that as well. I was starting to become good at PTSD, and I didn't even know what it was.

The Real World

One single truth

One time again, I find pain is my friend
It has taught me the things I know
Oh, I've deluged it with booze
Chased shadows and followed the ruse
Searching for the right way to go

It has always been there, stares me in the eye
I marvel at the simplicity of it all
I'll shed a tear for friends who are dead
I'm prime for the rise and the fall

There is one single truth, above and beyond
Anything life has taught me
It's a living Jesus, who died on the cross
He died for our salvation you see

I live with the thought, it's there most days
I feel like I'm the one who cares
About blown away bodies and arms and such

And a burden I can no longer bear

So I turn it all over to the one single truth
And the tears on this page are witness
That Jesus is salvation and although I still hurt
Somehow he offers me bliss

Some say ignorance is bliss but not in this case
for experience has shaped me as man
I walk with dead bodies, in a month, in a year
Pray Jesus, lend me a hand

The Richard Nixon impeachment trial was like a popcorn-and-soda event for me. Nixon represented a pro-war establishment whose deceit was deadly to my veterans. Every day I took great pleasure at watching the trials progress on television. The year before, many in the Rogue Valley had taken part in a program called Dump One for Dick. All you had to do was take a dump in a plastic bag, pack it in a box, and mail it to the White House. We called him "Tricky Dick" and were giddy when he resigned on August 9, 1974.

This was another transition period for me. While in Vietnam we called the United States the "world." In the confined walls of academia, we called the rest of society, "The real world." I was about to begin part three in my quest to identify the world I would live in.

I had decided to attend a free university in the Minneapolis-Saint Paul area of Minnesota. The free university, ironically, cost a lot and offered a dual degree in community planning and sculpting that I found attractive. I had plans to finance the education with gold angel dust or work. My significant other, B. J., and I busied ourselves preparing for the trip.

B. J. provided our main source of income at the time as she had started a small business cleaning homes. In little more than a month she had to stop taking new customers because her schedule was full. B. J. worked hard and refused to raise her rates because she felt the prices were fair. She had no need for greed. I respected that attitude.

Al and his girlfriend wanted to make the trip with us. At first, the logic of pooling our resources seemed rational, but over time competing personalities and plans would send his van in one direction and mine in the other.

We set up temporary camp in our vans on a ridge within artillery range of downtown Minneapolis-Saint Paul. We looked for a place to rent for two days without much luck. On day three we called a group meeting to discuss our options. I wanted to cancel our mission and return to Oregon while we still had resources. I knew I could get work in Oregon.

The group decided to go in opposite directions. Al's van would continue east while B. J. and I returned to Oregon. My mother put us up until I found work and bought a small piece of property.

Alcohol had been creeping into my life in a destructive way for many years. I started drinking every day, just a little more than the budget allowed. This is when I started to pick up some serious clues about the impact that the Vietnam experiences would have on my everyday life. I started hanging around with the guys who worked at the same lumber mill as I did. I was looking for my Vietnam buddies, but they weren't here. The people around me could never match up to the grunts in the bush. The mill workers didn't match up to my standards either, and, not surprisingly, neither could I.

B. J. and I started having children. I faced a roadblock constructed of a gigantic philosophic barrier. I hated what the corporate domination of American foreign policy had done to my veterans in Vietnam. I did not see hope in the future and concluded that bringing a child into this world would be an act of cruelty. Like most men, I wanted to give my children everything, but I had so little. B. J. was wiser about these things and instinctively knew that once the child was born, we would find a way to make it work.

At the end of the day, I had to give in to my belief that the decision to have a baby was B. J.'s. It was her body and, even though we were together, she must make the final decision on the birth of a child. It was her body.

Away from home, at work and at play, I had looming battles of my own. The demons of war had crippled me socially. I had been raised, like all my other brothers, with a weapon in my hands. Before I had reached legal hunting age, I was allowed to use the single shot .22 rifle at will or at least when it was not in use by one of my brothers. My best friend, Tuffy, and I did some crazy things with our .22s. The most dangerous was when we staged a firefight with live rounds.

As I have mentioned, Tuffy served with the First Cavalry Division in Vietnam for one year before receiving a terrible burn on his chest and neck. Fate would have us stationed in Fort Hood, Texas, at the same time in 1967. He would show me how to smoke weed. I was a good student. Tuffy wrote a poem about Vietnam and shared it with me. I in turn will share it in this writing.

Just another Gook

Many years ago I found myself in a very foreign land
Sweat and dirt on face and arms, a weapon in my hand.

At my feet there lay another, he was dying but he tried
to reach into his black pajamas, but in his effort he had died.

I knelt and found what he was looking for in oil covered canvas sack.

When I saw what was inside it I wished that I could put it back.

Three faces peered out at me from the picture in my hand
His Momma and his wife were there with bare feet in the sand.

A small child held in its mother's arms beckoned their father home.

But his father lay there at my feet, his mouth dripped blood and foam.

I was sorry I had done this but it was him or me
what the hell was I doing here in this land across the sea.

I shook the picture from my mind and dropped it on his chest
He was just another Gook, just like all the rest.

But as I walked on I faltered and tears came to my eyes
Or was it sweat that dripped there, the sweat of all G.I.s

Why were my legs a trembling? It was probably only fear
for in a war, in any war, one's own life is dear
I went on.

Donald Leslie
A Company, First Battalion
First Airborne Brigade
First Cavalry Division
An Khe, Vietnam

The consequences of my tour in Vietnam would overlap and neutralize the long family tradition of big-game hunting. The first time I shot a squirrel after returning to the world I turned into an emotional mess. For the next ten years I would not own a weapon and could not kill a fish on the end of the line or a flower in a field. I tried several times over the years to reestablish the connection with hunting, but none worked. I tried the traditional hunt with a rifle, but when I killed a deer my mood turned sour. I switched to hunting with a bow with the logic that it would make the hunt more equal, only to have the required stalking bring on flashbacks. On my last attempt, I tried to hunt elk with a .357 magnum pistol. It was super spooky, and I quit for the last time. It is confusing: If you fuck with me, I might plan to stalk you and burn your home, but I will not kill anything unless it is necessary to survive. I respect nature, but humanity to me represents a stain on the earth bloated by its own self-importance and vanity about its relationship to God.

The Fourth of July celebration and parade is a big deal in rural Eastern Oregon. We honor and celebrate our independence with bands, parades, and fireworks. We hold barbecues fun games for the kids and lots of beer. It had never occurred to me that the celebration would be a source of contention that would begin a twenty-year trend.

A small group of friends joined B. J. and me on the sidewalk of Main Street. We waited for the parade of horses, a band, rodeo queen, and floats to pass by. The first horse that arrived had an American flag at the end of a long stanchion. The lines of people on the sidewalk stood to salute or place a hand over their hearts as a sign of respect for the flag. I had been standing on the sidewalk with my small group of friends. As the flag approached, my friends put a hand over their heart in respect while I sat down and refused to honor the flag that had deceived and killed my veterans.

As a high school athlete, I would choke up when the national anthem played at the beginning of each football or basketball game. As a combat veteran, I had lost respect for our flag. The war in Vietnam had challenged my respect and replaced it with contempt. I would not rise to honor the flag for another twenty years.

Time and circumstance brought me to a high school football game many years later in Grant County where I stood alone on a dimly lit highway shoulder as the national anthem signaled the beginning of the contest. I came to attention and saluted the flag, much to my surprise. I discovered that I had no further need to boycott a tradition I held my heart on. The contempt I had developed for authority and tradition had influenced my actions for twenty years. I could once again honor the flag for my own reasons and at my own choosing. If I decide to fly my personal flag at night, it will be lighted properly, as it should be. If the light goes out, the flag comes down at sunset with honor. There are many dark flags across the nation that should be taken down at sunset; people disrespect rules and fly the flag without a dedicated light. Take a walk around your block after dark and see how many people treat the flag with contempt.

B. J. and I had one baby boy and were working on a second child when I quit my job in the saw mill to take a lower paying job as the manpower planner for the Comprehensive Employment and Training Act (CETA) program in a two-county area in Southeast Oregon. I was an employee of a political subdivision called the Southeast Oregon Council of Governments, (SEOCOG). The SEOCOG was composed of elected officials from both Harney and Malheur counties. Mayors, county judges, and county sheriffs served on the board. Agency heads and city council members also had a seat.

The organization's staff director was a Vietnam veteran who had served with the First Cavalry Division. We knew very little about each other's tours partly because we were still trying to understand what had happened over there. We had many other things to do, and Vietnam was creeping but not yet visible. Our fields of fire were not adequate to protect us from the trauma.

When I met the director, he sat on top of a two-county organization that included the home weatherization program, the comprehensive land use plan, the CETA program with an annual budget of approximately four hundred thousand dollars, grant writing for items covered under the Law Enforcement Assistance Administration (LEAA), and housing and urban development. If memory serves, the CETA program created three hundred full-time and part-time employment opportunities in a two-county area every year.

One of the most interesting, to me, and educational projects we developed while employed as planners concerned the future of the area's economy. We had six students and one professor from Southern Oregon College come to Harney County for this research project. I posed a hypothetical situation to the group and allowed them one week to gather data. They would then return to

Southern Oregon where they would transform the research into a paper.

The hypothetical question was: if sustained yield of our timber resources is ignored and unrestricted harvesting continues at the current rate, what will be the short- and long-term consequences for Harney County?

It was easy to conclude that the county had a singular economic base almost totally reliant on timber harvesting and production. I was aware that sustained yield was being exceeded by more than one hundred million board feet a year. I was also aware of the political and corporate influences on this policy.

Individuals and small groups of students fanned out to begin collecting information from agencies and organizations throughout the county. I kept two students behind for a private conversation about a special project within the larger assignment. They would cap off their week by interviewing the head of the largest lumber company in this part of the state. I would provide the researchers with some juicy information very few people knew or cared about.

The rest of the group would dig into the agriculture of the area and provide a detailed history of the Edward Hines Lumber Company and the role of private and governmental agencies in the county's future.

My father had worked as a truck driver for the Hines Lumber Company for more than thirty-two years. My siblings and I were raised in a company-owned town and lived in a company-owned house. We bought our food in a company-owned store, and my dad got drunk at a company-owned bar. We also used company-owned tokens as a form of credit and went swimming in a company-owned pool. It was about time I learned something about the company.

Edward Hines was born in 1863. Like most kids of his time, he went to work at an early age. By the time he was fourteen, he had a full-time job at a Chicago lumberyard. When he turned twenty-one, he was promoted to secretary-treasurer in that same lumber-yard with the S. K. Martin lumber firm. In 1892 he started his own business with two friends and fellow employees of the S. K. Martin firm. Hines was very successful and by 1896 bought out S. K. Martin, his first employer. Hines had the personality of a successful salesman and developed a lifelong friendship with Frederick Weyerhaeuser, who would sit on the Hines board of directors and own shares in the company.

Hines bought mills and purchased two hundred million feet of Wisconsin timber from Weyerhaeuser & Rutledge. These purchases were soon followed by acquiring an additional three hundred million board feet of timber. With growth in mind, Hines next purchased three billion board feet of southern pine in the Badger State.

Known as the Bear Valley Unit, the large Oregon tract of USDA timberland, near Seneca, Oregon, was laid out in 1922 by the US Forest Service. It was first sold to Fred Herrick in 1923, but Herrick defaulted on his contract with the forest service and Hines acquired rights to the unit's 67,400 acres of land containing an estimated 890 million board feet of timber. It has been called the Martin Exchange, and it would allow Hines to buy timber off the land deeded to the forest service at a reduced stumpage. The timber on every other section of land retained by Hines would be free. This arrangement was wrapped in the concept that the government and the corporation could share firefighting responsibility for the combined total of all the purchased land. At a specified date, all the land would be deeded over to the government.

One of the goals of the forest service was to improve rail connections between national lumber markets and the Blue

Mountain forests of Eastern Oregon. After winning the timber contract, the Hines Company built the fifty-two-mile Oregon and Northwestern Railroad between Burns and Seneca and the timber that lay mostly east of there. Timber cutting from the Bear Valley Unit continued through 1968. At one point Edward Hines would own tracts of timbered land from Canada to Mexico.

In the late 1990s I would help use 1,500 pounds of explosive product to collapse the train tunnel between Seneca and Burns on the Oregon and Northwestern railway line.

The research students became aware that the specified expiration date of the Martin Exchange was only a few years away from their planned interview with the local company manager. The questions I asked the students to pursue were: What impact will the termination of the Martin Exchange have on the Edward Hines Lumber Company operations in Eastern Oregon? Will they stay? Will they leave? What is the future forecast for the communities dependent on the jobs associated with Edward Hines?

Not surprisingly, the response from the local manager being interviewed was that the expiration of the Martin Exchange would have zero impact on their operations. Two years later Hines shut down the mill in the town bearing its name. Within five years of the questions from the students, Edward Hines had sold all its holdings and moved back to Chicago.

The students took the information back to Southern Oregon and delivered a finished report about two months later. When I attempted to introduce the paper into the community, it seemed that there was little interest among elected officials and agency heads. They didn't want to talk about it. Perhaps it was too large of a concept to engage mentally. Grant County to the north had seen the writing on the wall and was fully addressing and implementing elements of their comprehensive land use plans for the future.

Harney County didn't seem to be willing to accept the reports of possible future changes in the economic base.

My boss and friend accepted a job offer as a planner in another part of the state, and I notified my college roommate/friend Mike about the opening. Mike applied and was hired as the director of SEOCOG. I stayed in my position as manpower planner and took on additional duties in grant writing and planning. I still know where all the federal money is, but I only search the files for legal jurisdictions with a compelling agenda. I would never get it for myself; that's not who I am.

The best things seem to happen by themselves. A small old mining community close to the junction of the Idaho, Oregon, and Nevada state lines asked me to help it get a fire truck for a volunteer fire department. I drove to the little town with paper and a pencil. A mining company had recently reactivated a dormant claim in hopes of taking advantage of the soaring gold prices. The city council and fire department felt compelled to address insurance issues as a result of recent formal incorporation activities. I can't for the life of me remember the name of that town. It makes no difference.

I collected enough information from city hall to establish a modest number I could use as in-kind matching funds in the search for a fire truck. The next day I made a phone call to the Oregon surplus equipment manager. I introduced myself and told the director I was looking for a fire truck with equipment for a small rural mining town in Southeast Oregon. The director informed me that he had to leave town on business, but he assured me that he would contact me as soon as possible.

Two days later I was on the phone with the same surplus items director. He said he had just received a fire truck with equipment. He said we could have the fire truck if we could get a lowboy to transport it as the truck had a top speed of forty-five miles per hour on the open road. The lowboy was no problem for a community where both mining and ranching dictated the use of big trucks and trailers for taking cattle to market or transporting large equipment into the mine.

The next item on the list was training. How do you train someone to operate a fire truck and/or fight structural fires? I presented this problem to the Southeast Oregon Council of Governments board of directors. They decided to use some CETA program monies to pay volunteers for taking fire department training. We also found additional surplus equipment and the funds to purchase supplies for the fire truck we could not obtain through the government surplus program.

The best part of the fire department project was that it all came together so easily, almost as if it were meant to happen. It had a will of its own. I didn't do that much to make the whole program come together. It was meant to happen. What are the odds of making a phone call and finding a free fire truck with equipment? It was meant to happen.

In order to have full access to the broad range of government-sponsored programs, rural areas with low populations must jump through many hoops. One of those hoops is called a consortium. A consortium is when two or more legal jurisdictions band together in a political subdivision that represents a population of one hundred thousand people or more. These one hundred thousand people can then qualify for grants and programs that were previously unavailable. Mike viewed the administrative body in the northern part of the state as the best host for our consortium needs. I wanted to form our own administrative body instead of farming it out to someone I didn't know or trust. Mike won the argument, and the SEOCOG board of directors supported his plan. The result was that we were both out of a job within a year.

I went to work as a knot bumper for a scab logging outfit in Northern Idaho for a while. "Scab" is a slang word that means "private, nonunion." It was a father-son-son outfit. They were all crazy, get-out-of-their-way, angry loggers. B. J. worked as a special education instructor at a day care center and later started a preschool for her friends with children the same age as ours.

The owner of the nonunion logging outfit in Northern Idaho was stoned out of his mind every day. Years earlier he had injured himself in a logging accident. Accidents and stupidity can sometimes be the same thing; just ask the grunts who shoot their buddies accidentally. Every single day after the accident, he would take massive doses of painkillers for phantom pains. The injury screwed up his back, so he couldn't rotate his head far enough to look behind him.

The most dangerous place I have ever been was the landing where the boss was depositing logs that would be stacked into large decks. The boss would bounce down the hill on his rubber-tired skidder intent on turning 180 degrees, release the grapples to dump the load, and head back up the hill to collect more logs without ever stopping. I admired his intent, but the reality was dangerously different.

I realized that the boss was stoned out of his mind every day running from the phantom pain demons. Sometimes the boss would arrive at the landing with no logs in the grapples. He didn't know any different because his injuries would not allow him to turn around and look behind him. He would do the 180-degree turn, pull the lever to release the phantom logs, counting the phantom money he would make when he delivered the phantom logs to the phantom mill. For all I know, he had phantom sex with his phantom wife.

If by chance he would have logs in the grapple, things would get real dangerous real fast. He would do the 180-degree turn lifting the logs off the ground. Even a small log will kill you, and the boss could create flying logs that were moving at forty miles an hour. I found it hard to find a safe place on the landing. His oldest son was just as crazy and would eventually smash himself up while working in the woods.

After Mike bargained away our jobs to the Eastern Oregon Consortium, I quit the logging job to help him renovate a house he had bought near the Idaho border. Our wives moved to Portland and set up a community house. Mike and I joined the ladies a few months later after he had sold the property. We got a contract that involved rescuing injured dogs and cats on the streets of Portland and taking them to a twenty-four-hour veterinarian. Two families in one house created a great amount of pressure, so B. J. and I found a place of our own.

B. J. was accepted in an apprenticeship program as a pipe fitter on the docks in Portland. She made big money and I became a stay-at-home dad. Few men have the opportunity to care for their children full time. There is great joy and love in this activity and so much to learn and appreciate. I would struggle all day to feed the children, change diapers, get them to school on time, and prepare dinner. And just when I had them calmed down in the late afternoon, B. J. would come in the door and jack the kids up to a high pitch again.

After a while I started officiating basketball games for the Portland city league to make what turned out to be drinking money. I did 101 games over a thirteen-week period my first year as a Portland city league basketball official. On some days I would do two golden ball league games of six-year-olds at noon followed by two church league games of high school youth at 4:00 p.m. At eight that night I would do two city league drink-beer-and-play games with adults who never grew up. I did many of these games alone, which sometimes prompted me to carry a concealed weapon in my car. One night members of both teams followed me to my car after I had stopped the game and declared both teams the losers.

B. J. and I decided to end our relationship. Every day hundreds of men on the docks hooted and whistled when she passed telling her the things I wasn't. We fought for a year before deciding to split custody of the two boys.

I was a full-blown alcoholic by this time. I was massively confused by my experiences in Vietnam and unimpressed by the results of my anti-war activities. My inability to make life work in the world did not concern me. I was practicing risky behavior on a regular basis and perfecting antisocial techniques without a clue that I was doing it.

Once again I would find myself back in Eastern Oregon country, but this time I was a single parent. I had been reaching for the bottom of a trauma-induced emotional trap, and I was being successful at acts of self-destruction. I was a single parent, and my oldest child lived with me for six years before he begged me to let him live with his mother.

As a single parent, I was living on less than the take-home pay of a one-legged chicken. The lumber mills and logging operations had curtailed their operations years before. The only work was part time and low paying. I had to apply for welfare for a couple of months. This was my financial bottom, and I pushed all roadblocks aside in order to change things.

The National Guard presented me with an opportunity to keep the sergeant E-5 rank I had achieved while in the regular army.

The income from one weekend a month and two weeks a year training increased my annual income by twenty-five percent. Joining the guard also gave me the opportunity to retrain myself in the use of weapons. I had gone ten years without touching a weapon and I needed to break that boycott. The guard had lots of weapons to train on.

I became a member of an armored cavalry unit with tanks and APCs. They made me a track commander of an M113 armored personnel carrier. The National Guard at this time was overweight and alcoholic. Some of the leaders had joined the National Guard to keep from being drafted and sent to Vietnam. They liked it enough to attend officer candidate school, and when I met them they were high on themselves.

Vietnam had left a bitter taste in my mouth for authority figures and wannabe leaders who never showed up for combat. The troop leaders were graded on personnel attendance and numbers of people who either joined or reenlisted. The weekend training schedule was geared toward having a good time and protecting the drunks. I was one of the drunks.

When I served in the guard, I observed that very few in the section know their skill level one tasks. A skill level one task is something every private in the military is tested on annually. It is a basic knowledge skill that every sergeant E-5 must train his subordinates in. Every sergeant worth his salt will have a fifteen-minute skill level one class in his pocket at all times. The troop leaders I met in the guards could not encode and decode a nuclear, biological, and chemical (NBC) message. They could not breach a minefield or call for and adjust artillery fire, and their map reading would have been a joke if they had any maps to read from.

The field tactics were juvenile, and I believed that if you trained to die you would be successful. Every M60A1 tank gunner in the troop could get a first-round hit on a target at 1,500 meters, but our formations put us in a straight line—of tank, APC, tank, APC—like we were holding hands and all less than fifty yards apart. Command did not use scouts to scout, and they had no notion of partnering up an APC with a tank as cover. These are the kinds of tactics that kill my veterans in war while gaining career opportunities for others.

The one weekend a month was a buildup to the two-week summer camp where our skills could be tested. I kept my mouth shut for the first year to see which way the wind blew. On my first day of summer camp, the truth was revealed. We convoyed from the motorpool at Gowen Field to the training area two hours away. When we reached our night defensive position (NDP), I jumped off the track and began using my compass to orient myself because this was new country to me. The platoon sergeant laughed at my use of a compass to determine direction and stated he knew what direction north was because he had been here a dozen times before. I asked him to point to the north, and he responded by pointing to the east. When I informed him of his mistake, he countered by saying my compass was wrong. I would find out over the next two days that my platoon sergeant did not know how to call for fire, use a compass, or read a map. As a matter of fact, there was not a single map in the entire scout section. No one called for fire unless they needed to light a cigarette. Why have a map and compass when you don't know how to use them?

The next year I volunteered to be in the advance party for summer camp so I could find and acquire proper maps for everyone in the scout section. I also started rebelling against the training regimen laid out by higher-higher. One weekend a month, I ran my crew through the scheduled training in 25 percent of the allotted time. I then opened up my personal training schedule for the rest of the weekend.

My schedule was combat oriented. We practiced calling for fire over the PRC-25 radio. We then disassembled, assembled, and function checked the .45 pistol, the M16 rifle, the M60 machine gun, and the Ma-deuce, or .50 caliber machine gun. Later, after I was promoted to staff sergeant E-6 and became the scout section leader, I took the scouts into the surrounding hills on weekends to run foot patrols. I prepared for these foot patrols by collecting simulated booby traps, artillery rounds, and hundreds of rounds of M60 and M16 blank ammo from the stash in summer camp. I trained the track commanders to set booby traps in front of their night defensive position (NDP). I also instituted a "hot bed" policy. During summer camp I instructed each track commander to be prepared for twenty-four-hour days by having one person asleep on the hot bed at all times. That person would be in charge of our NDP giving us the upper hand over other sleep-deprived combatants.

Proper radio procedure in our unit was nonexistent. The general rule is never to send a message that lasts for more than four seconds. Longer messages make it easier to pinpoint the location of the sender and bring damn-damn down on their sorry asses. Everyone had a radio, but few in the guard used them properly. I cut through a lot of bullshit by doing two things: I gave independent call signs to key people in the unit. The troop commanding officer was not on that list. My personal call sign was "Foxtrot," which came from my tour in Vietnam. I called another track commander "Kilo" because he was a couple of pounds overweight. "Whiskey" was the call sign of a heavy drinker, and "Hotel" was the call sign of the section leader's driver. These were phonetic alphabet call signs.

I also developed "jump frequencies." I was no doubt a pain in the ass for management. Each day in the field, I issued an alternate frequency to the official one handed down from higher-higher. Military radios have a high and low band. Higher-higher designated a certain frequency, and I issued an alternate secret frequency for private conversations and secret tactical use by enlisted personnel in the scout section. When I wanted our people to go to the alternate frequency, I said on the radio, "Black six, this is Foxtrot, I have you Lima Charlie, over." My scout section switched frequencies when they heard me call "Black six" with a fake communication check. The alternate frequency would be simple, like flip-flop plus one or flip-flop minus two. The scout section would hear me call "Black six" and switch to either the high or low band depending on the official band that day. The scouts would flip-flop the bands on their radios to add or subtract numbers depending on our agreement. This was a great way to gather a quick consensus among the scouts. We could bitch or develop grunt tactics among ourselves and higher-higher couldn't find us.

By "develop tactics" I mean trick-fuck higher-higher into doing the sensible thing. Commanders in the unit dropped the ball when it came to NBC training. The leaders would not schedule the annual movement oriented protective posture (MOPP) training in the wintertime because, frankly, it made sense. They would schedule our MOPP training when the temperature was 110 degrees at Gowen Field. We would be in full MOPP IV status, which included face mask, rubber gloves, and boots plus the charcoal-lined head-to-toe protective gear. MOPP IV also required us to button up our vehicles, which increased the temperature by more than I care to think. Every summer camp they did this, and people would start to go down with heat exhaustion.

The advantages of doing MOPP IV training during winter exercises at the home base are obvious. You are able to focus on the subject at hand without other concerns diverting your attention. NBC is a complicated series of procedures that demands time, training, and effort. Individuals remaining in MOPP IV for extended periods of time during the cold of winter have reduced anxiety reactions from the claustrophobic protective gear because of practiced familiarity. Trainees in MOPP IV status, without the adverse effects of heatstroke, can practice firing personal weapons, installing, retrieving, assembling, disassembling, and function checking the automatic chemical alarm detection kit and other skills needed to achieve the mission. Students also have the time to become aware of the shortcomings associated with US practices regarding NBC warfare.

When military units become familiar with possible conditions they will encounter, they are more likely to survive. If you train to die, then you will die. If you train to train, then everybody wins. The MOPP IV charcoal-lined suits will only absorb chemicals for four to five hours in a contaminated environment before you have to change them. The difficult procedures of changing a contaminated suit in a contaminated environment must be laid out and rehearsed, or things will not go well. If you don't want to glow, then you got to know.

The next summer camp, higher-higher repeated the 110-degree charcoal-sponsored MOPP-till-you-drop exercise. They declared a MOPP IV situation, so I buttoned up our track and waited about fifteen minutes. I then asked my crew who wanted to fake a case of heat exhaustion so we could end this dangerous exercise. I coached the volunteer because I had seen a lot of heat exhaustion in Vietnam. We lowered the back ramp and took the casualty to the shady side of the track, where he removed his shirt and assumed a prone position. Another crew member used his canteen to pour water over the recruit to cool him down. If anyone came over to check, he was to act slow and groggy while complaining about having a bad headache.

Within fifteen minutes of my casualty report, an officer came by my APC to verify. The volunteer put on a good show, and soon everyone in the troop was ordered to end the MOPP exercise. Higher-higher may rule, but the grunts can fool the rule to make it cool.

It did not matter how long I traveled or how far I went, I could not escape the intrusive mental images and thoughts generated by my tour in combat. I had hoped that joining the National Guard would help me walk away from the trauma of Vietnam. After several years in the guard, I didn't have much hope left.

During one summer camp, I pushed myself way to hard. I was everywhere doing everything. At one point I stayed on my feet for thirty-six hours straight running foot patrols and achieving the scout section missions. At the end of summer camp, when we were processing our equipment, I had a major flashback. I tried to find a priest who wouldn't care if I had a disdain for organized religion and who knew something about PTSD. Having no luck at finding a priest, I sought out another Vietnam veteran. The CO found another Vietnam veteran willing to talk to me. The vet and I spent the rest of the day together and, after he told me his story about getting drunk and naked in the woods the year before with the barrel of his rifle in his mouth, we became friends. I was looking for someone to talk to, someone who understood. If this guy was going to eat a bullet, I was sure we were in the same mess hall if not the same table.

I was struggling to keep afloat when the US Forest Service offered me a seasonal job marking timber. The employment with the forest service was the first step to putting my life together. I went to work on the timber-marking crew from March through November. Beginning in August I signed up for training programs through the National Guard. I made more money attending these National Guard schools than I could if I had collected unemployment.

One of the classes I signed up for was the tank commander's course at Gowen Field near Boise, Idaho. I had been inside of a tank when stationed at Fort Hood, Texas, in 1967, but that was about all I knew or remembered. All of the instructors in the course were master tank commanders. They knew every detail of every element about the M60A1 tank. At the end of the two-week course, each student was required to pass nineteen different skills that ranged from bore sighting the main gun to replacing the firing pin in the breach block. The skills test also included the disassembly, assembly, and function check of the .50 caliber and 7.62 coaxial plus the handheld .45 caliber pistol and .45 caliber grease gun.

During the end of the class skills test, I passed seventeen tasks the first go-around; I couldn't remember ever having trained on one particular skill and missed the time limit on another one. I passed the remaining two skills on the second of three allowed attempts. I attribute all my success in this class to the master tank commander instructors. This was an excellent class taught by expert people who achieved fantastic results. Two other people from my home unit who had been tank commanders for more than eight years took the course with me. They both failed because they thought they knew it all and therefore didn't pay attention. My tank was empty. I entered the class with an open agenda and let the experts fill me up.

The noncommissioned officer's course was required for anyone planning to be promoted from sergeant E-5 to staff sergeant E-6. The training took place at Camp Rilea on the Oregon coast. My behavior was totally self-destructive but just barely manageable. I got drunk every night but made sure the squad I was assigned to would have the maximum success at every aspect of the field training. The last segment of the training cycle was a thirty-six-hour romp through the woods where each student would lead the squad on a mission. I walked point for each newly selected squad leader. I would run unarmed solo deep recons, find and fix the enemy, and help the squad leader plan a hasty attack.

At the end of the training cycle, I would have been chosen first in the class had I voted for myself instead of someone else. I told the class I didn't need the recognition because I knew who I was and what I could do. The person I basically gave the first-place award to wanted and needed it, but he was not a good leader the men would follow even though he wanted it so badly. We took a physical fitness test on the last day of training. I was about forty years old at the time, but I was the only person in our squad of twenty-year-olds to max the test. I was a drink-all-night and run-all-day fool.

The advanced noncommissioned officer's course was held at Fort Beauregard, Louisiana. This course was required for persons seeking promotion to platoon sergeant E-7. I passed the course but dropped out of the National Guard to attend a six-week-long alcohol treatment before being promoted to platoon sergeant. I also took the small-arms instructor's course, which certified me as a range master.

I took further advantage of the training opportunities to visit Fort Irwin, California, and fight with the Opposition Force (OP4) for nineteen days. Fort Irwin is the home of the National Training Center. Units all over the world stand in line for the opportunity to take a shot at the OP4. The OP4 personnel wear soviet uniforms, use soviet weapons and tactics, and drive visually modified (vismod) equipment. To build visually modified equipment, the mechanics would weld steel to the sides of an old Sherman tank that was cut to resemble a soviet BMP or tank.

The National Training Center guys were good. Some of the personnel in the OP4 had never been trained in or practiced American tactics. They ate, slept, dressed, and dreamed soviet.

They also schooled some of the best infantry and armored military units in the United States. While I was there, I fought against the Second Infantry Division. I fucked them up one afternoon by calling in a fire mission on the landing zone they were using to conduct a combat assault by helicopter. The fire mission produced many casualties and forced the unit to alter its plans and take a different route to its target. At the end of my nineteen-day tour, the First Battalion of the Seventy-Third Armor, Bunker Busters, awarded me a signed certificate of achievement and a soviet-style winter hat complete with a big red star that I still wear to this day.

The National Training Center is famous for the technology it has adopted. Every person and piece of equipment is tracked at a headquarters building far removed from the field. They do this using the multiple integrated laser engagement system (MILES). They have a giant screen in the headquarters building that shows the location of every vehicle and person in the training area. If one tank shoots another, they know it at headquarters. If there is a dispute, they are the judges and are never wrong. Fort Irwin is the home of a world-class training center.

The crew I hooked up with was hot. They went to work around noon locating the enemy and developing plans. They attacked between ten and twelve at night and went to ground at first light. They hooked up with the rest of their unit around 0800 to eat and sleep for a few hours before returning to the fight. The training offered at this facility would save many lives in the upcoming Desert Storm, Operation Enduring Freedom, and Operation Iraqi Freedom wars.

In the early 1980s, I got a seasonal job with the US Forest Service that was located in a small town with a very active Vietnam veterans group. During my first month on the job, I saw a newspaper ad encouraging Vietnam veterans to join a therapy group. I wrote a letter to the Center for Human Development rambling on about how getting shot was better than being blown up. I signed the note "Foxtrot" before I put it in the mailbox.

A couple of weeks later, I stopped in at the community center to have a look around. One of the counselors approached me and introduced himself as Dan, a marine combat veteran. Dan and I started a relationship that day that lasted longer than most I have had. Dan asked me a couple of questions and then suddenly said, "Are you Foxtrot?" I flinched upright and responded with something like, "You must have read my letter." Dan took charge by telling the receptionist to hold all calls and inviting me into his office for some chitchat. We talked for about thirty minutes before Dan asked if I would like to join his combat veterans group. The two words "combat veterans" brought me on board. I agreed to return in one week to undergo a formal intake and evaluation. Dan and the Center for Human Development became a key element in helping me regain some leverage in my life.

The first Vietnam veteran I met in the group was Budd. Budd had been a brown water sailor in Vietnam, and his father had been a lifer on submarines and spent time in a Japanese POW camp during WWII. A brown water sailor is a person in the navy who operates or mans patrol boat river (PBR) in the brown waters inland from the South China Sea. These fast, agile, and heavily armed fiberglass shallow draft vessels worked often with the Ninth Infantry Division as well as with Navy SEAL teams.

Budd is one of the most charming people I have ever met. He is a wonderfully rounded navy brat. He could walk into any bar in the world and leave hours later with two new best friends. Budd is also one of the most unstable people I have ever met also and a somewhat reluctant lifelong friend. He is the reason why people should believe that PTSD exists and needs to be treated. I can't tell you the best stories about Budd because most of them might be illegal and/or unethical, immoral, and depraved. One minute he would be solid as a rock, and the next minute he would disable my vehicle so I would wreck my car and die. Budd was funny that way.

The seasonal job with the forest service allowed me to pay my bar bills and rent a shit-hole apartment within walking distance of my job. The hard work of marking timber was this alcoholic's perfect excuse to drink lots of beer every night, weekends, two days a month plus two weeks a year. I was burning the candle at both ends and trying to light the middle with a block of C-4 explosive. "Blow me up" was my vision of success. Gone at last, gone at last, good God almighty I'm gone at last.

The rap group met once a week. Budd and I would get together at the local bar for an hour before and after the meeting, in direct violation of the rules. I never talked about the personal issues I brought home from Vietnam while in group. I listened and responded to everyone else whenever they had a crisis, but I didn't know where to begin at addressing my issues.

Another breakthrough came when Dan and the Center for Human Development sponsored a visit from the one-half-size replica of the Vietnam Veterans Memorial wall. The wall came to me because at the time I had no intention of going to the wall. It pissed me off when people said, "Welcome home," because in my mind they were twenty years late. They held a parade in New York to honor the Vietnam Veterans, and it was twenty years late also. Where were these people when I was humping the bush? They offered to shake my hand twenty years late because they wanted to sell something or brag about knowing a veteran. If they cared they would have showed up in my foxhole in Vietnam.

By the time they had the wall set up at the Grant County Fairgrounds, I was a crumbling emotional mess. I had bunkered up big time and couldn't move. Budd showed up at my place with beer that I didn't need but quickly drank. I tried to walk out my front door dozens of times to no avail. Sometime around 2:00 a.m. I embarked on a one-man nighttime patrol to scout the wall. I moved from shadow to shadow, evading contact and avoiding people. I got within thirty yards of the display and set up an OP (observation post). I melted into the shadows with a building at my back. I became confused about what to do next.

A military-age female, floating on luminescent air between her feet and the ground, carried lighted candles in her eyes and had her head on a swivel. Having spotted me in the shadows, she approached with the gentle persuasion of a cat's purr and allowed me to divorce the shadow dance and travel the last thirty yards to meet the dead. My breathing was deep and heavy, and I lost all ability to talk. She magically drifted away as soon as we could see the wall, and I realized my dilemma: I did not remember the names of my dead. I could tell you how they died, I could describe the severed limbs and position of the body, I could tell you where the booby trap was that killed them and the sound of a sucking chest wound. I could tell you the direction I was facing, but I didn't know the names of my dead. I had gotten within five yards of the wall, but it would take me another twenty years to get close enough to touch it. I didn't know their names.

I exited the building through the back door and started shadow jumping toward my apartment. I heard a loud noise off to my left and saw another member of our Vietnam veteran's therapy group using a 2x4 and rocks to beat a wooden fence panel to death while he yelled and cried. I didn't feel so alone after that.

The veterans group showed me that there was hope. Lots of veterans from Vietnam had problems readjusting to the world. More than sixty-three thousand Vietnam veterans had eaten a bullet, kissed a train, or done an Evel Knievel off a cliff in their car. Other veterans did suicide by cop or drank until they drowned and smoked until they choked. It was not just me; I was not the only one acting crazy. I found comfort in realizing that the pain was broadly spread among Vietnam veterans. Someone in the rap group would point at me and say how screwed up I was while I pointed at someone else to bring attention to how messed up he was. In this group, if you were civilian normal you didn't belong. I would later learn that we were normal people having normal reactions to abnormal events.

I heard several people in the group repeat a combat veteran's mantra: PTSD is chronic, progressive, and incurable. I found this belief to be both interesting and inaccurate. How would they know PTSD is incurable unless they had spoken to every traumatized individual on the planet? A gap existed between the accepted mantra about PTSD and a full understanding of the subject. Many years later the missing part of the mantra was exposed to me. PTSD is chronic and progressive unless you do something about it. And what you can do is manage the symptom; that's about the best you can hope for at this time. Your goal cannot be to cure PTSD. Experts have tried to achieve that for generations, and they have used pills, electric shock, and surgery to no avail. The best you can hope for is to manage the symptoms. This must be an individually tailored long-term program of recovery.

After four years of working seasonal for the US Forest Service in the late '80s, I applied for a full-time permanent position. The veteran's preference pushed me to the head of the list, which made a lot of nonveterans jealous. They called us roster-blocking veterans. They could not climb up the roster because a privileged veteran was blocking the way. Many in the forest service resented the veterans, but they were forced to follow the bureaucracy rules. Plus, I was one hell of a good worker if you forgave the occasional freak-out.

I knew that I would never be able to hold on to the permanent full-time position in the forest service unless I quit drinking. I called a meeting with my boss and worked out a plan to attend a six-week alcohol and drug treatment program at the veteran's hospital in Roseburg, Oregon. The only mistake I made was to schedule the treatment program for February when the workload for the forest service was at its lowest. A friend told me I should go to treatment ASAP because waiting would give me too much time to drink the state dry. I should have listened to her. Man, was she ever right. Before February arrived Oregon had to borrow beer from Idaho just to make it through the month.

The rules at the veterans A&D (alcohol and drug) treatment facility suggested that participants abstain from using their drug of choice beginning five days prior to checking in at the center. I planned to quit drinking so I could keep my job, and I followed their rules to the letter. Many years before, I had quit smoking weed because my anti-war activities and desire to bring my veterans home was more important than the smoke and joke with friends. Just as bringing my veterans home was more important than smoking weed in college, keeping the forest service job was more important than getting drunk. My class had eleven students; most of them had gotten drunk the night before arriving at the center. I was the only student who had not had a drink in five days. I felt like a fool, and the staff treated me with a great deal of suspicion because the norm, I would discover, was to party hardy until the A&D doors closed behind them. Everyone in my class was a veteran, but I was the only veteran with combat experience. More than 80 percent of the class was there as a result of a court mandate. They had been given the choice of A&D or jail. Most had been to jail and considered A&D a good alternative to confinement and the strong likelihood of a butt buddy.

I attacked the class head-on with full disclosure and a deep penetrating honesty rarely seen by the center staff. My approach was so open that the staff doubted my sincerity. I was extremely hungry for the available information, and I did not only my scheduled assignments but also the work for two others in the class. The instructors told us that of the eleven people in our class; only 30 percent would be sober at the end of one year. In five years only 10 percent of the original eleven alcoholics in our class would still be clean and sober.

We started the class with eleven people. The first two were sent home for bringing substances onto the A&D compound. One year after graduation only two of us remained sober.

My timber-marking crew boss, Larry, covered my ass all the way. He talked to the center staff over the phone about how he could help me when I returned to work. He made sure I had enough leave to cover my absence. He was the perfect boss. He did what someone in his position was supposed to, and I assure you that this is rare in a bureaucracy. He touched all the bases, and I owe him big time. He is on my winners list.

The A&D staff laid down some basic rules for dealing with possible stumbling blocks during our first minutes, months, and years of sobriety:

No. 1: Do not make any life-changing decisions during the first year of sobriety. Don't get married, don't move, don't get divorced or quit a job.

No. 2: Start a program of spiritual and mental health and stick to it.

No. 3: Don't congratulate yourself for being clean and sober until you have been clean for as long as you were drunk.

No. 4: More shall be revealed.

The first year of sobriety may have been the most difficult period of my life. Many of the thoughts and images that flooded my mind came out of the blue and smacked me alongside the head. I attended a forest service training session with a vanload of timber-related people one winter. The session was being held in a large city in the state of Washington. I hate cities as they make me feel closed in and vulnerable without adequate fields of fire.

The second day in town I got up between four and five in the morning and found a place to eat breakfast and read the newspaper. I read an article about an ex-marine Vietnam veteran who had been killed by the cops the day before somewhere in the state of Washington. The article stated that the marine was the only survivor when his platoon was overrun by NVA regulars in Vietnam. The people who knew him in high school said he was different when he returned home from the war. He moved into an abandoned shack up in the mountains and far from town. He lived alone and avoided contact with his family and friends. He said he didn't have any friends; he said all his friends were dead, and he considered them the lucky ones. The day before he had come out of the mountains and eaten breakfast at a small restaurant where everyone knew his name. After breakfast he went to his pickup and returned with his .357 magnum pistol and calmly killed two people. He then went back to his pickup and waited for the police to arrive. The police told him to put down his weapon, and he did just the opposite, forcing the police to kill him.

I lost it emotionally. I knew what he had done and why he done it. He had committed suicide by cop so he could join his dead buddies in the land of marine heroes. I contacted my tall, steady, and slow timber-marking crew boss who was also at the training session and let him know that I was fucked up. He gave me the freedom to phone my personal shrink, Dan, and contact a local veteran's crisis intervention center. I missed a day of training and felt humiliated and embarrassed about my personal crisis, but I was still alive at the end of the day. Not that being alive was anything that special.

After returning home I got together with Dan and later Budd. Between the three of us, we developed a strategy to deal with sudden trauma-induced behavior. Dan's contributions included: Do not bunker up and/or isolate yourself. Attend an AA meeting at a place you should locate when you first get into town. Budd introduced me to one of his tricks, which was always to carry a small piece of home with me whenever I traveled. I did this by putting some dirt from my yard in a plastic pill bottle. All of the advice helped. I still carry dirt in my travel kit.

One year after I sobered up, I saw a flyer from the US Forest Service Region 6 headquarters seeking persons who had been clean and sober for at least one year and were willing to bring a drug-free workplace program to their forest. I received permission from my boss to attend a weeklong training seminar on the Oregon coast. The seminar involved some training but was really more about the development and implementation of a region-wide drug-free workplace effort. I met lots of recovering people, and it seemed that most of them were Vietnam veterans. I knew I was in the right house.

I brought the program back to my home forest and started doing interventions, counseling, and planning an eye-opener drug and alcohol session for the next weeklong spring training exercise held each year on our forest. I did this with great discomfort, but I justified it by saying the information I had to give was more important than my personal comfort/safety. I did this many times in life, and it always reached a boiling point that caused me to have a meltdown. It was the same as walking point in Vietnam; I would make a target of myself for the good of the team, but there would come a time when I couldn't do it anymore.

A couple of years after developing the D&A program, I had an experience that would send me in a direction close to my heart and essential to my understanding of PTSD.

It was fire season and our timber-marking crew of six people had been dispatched to a lightning-caused fire in the northeast corner of our forest. A couple of hours after we arrived on the fire line, another frightened and exhausted four-person crew joined us from the wrong direction. They were breathing hard, sweating heavily, missing tools and equipment, and near panic. They had been sent to the wrong place, and the fire had overtaken them. Their packs containing food, clothes, and nighttime equipment had been eaten by a raging blowup on the fire line. These people had been traumatized, and I saw the looks of stressed-out combat veterans on their faces. If it had been up to me, I would have pulled that crew off the fire line and conducted a debriefing. The people in charge of the fire didn't even bother to replace the lost equipment let alone recognize the need for a debriefing.

The next time I was in the company of the regional director for the drug-free workplace program, I told him about the burnover incident and stressed my disappointment at the lack of a proper response from the forest service. He asked me why I didn't call him because he was also the director of the regional Critical Incident Stress Debriefing (CISD) program. He said he was preparing to train more people who were willing to conduct debriefings, and I was welcome to join. This presented me with another perfect opportunity to strap on a piece of plastic explosive and self-destruct, but I wouldn't find that out for another eight years.

Some of the first documented cases of traumatic stress, or what used to be called "transient situational disturbance" (TSD), can be traced to military combat. Research on the effectiveness of applied critical incident debriefing techniques has demonstrated that individuals who are provided CISD within a twenty-four- to seventy-two-hour period after the initial critical incident experience fewer short-term and long-term crisis reactions or less psychological trauma. Subsequently, emergency service workers, rescue workers, combat veterans, police and fire personnel, as well as the trauma survivors themselves who do not receive CISD, are at greater risk of developing many of the clinical symptoms.

My boss and the management above him agreed to allow me to become part of the regional debriefing team. The next year I attended a one-week training session and then waited for my opportunity to conduct a debriefing. The established procedure was to attend two debriefings as support. If that went well, the trainee would take the lead chair on the third debriefing with their mentor as support. I waited for more than a year before being dispatched to my first incident.

The message from the regional dispatcher said to meet the program director at the airport so we could fly to northern Oregon where a firefighting helicopter had crashed. I had seen crashed choppers in Vietnam, so familiarity was on my side. We conducted two debriefings over the next three days, but I don't remember much about them except that I passed the test.

The purpose of a debriefing was to address the long- and short-term psychological impact of a traumatic event on the victims and emergency responders. Emergency responders included police, fire, ambulance, dispatch, and medical professionals. Incidents that required special attention included decapitations, because they freaked most people out, and dead babies, because they freaked everyone out. Survivors often struggle to regain control of their lives. The countless others who have been traumatized by the critical event may eventually need professional attention and care for weeks, months, and possibly years afterward. The final extent of any traumatic situation may never be known or realistically estimated in terms of trauma, loss, and grief. In the aftermath of any critical incident, psychological reactions are quite common and fairly predictable. CISD can be a valuable tool following a traumatic event.

A critical incident is defined as a sudden death in the line of duty, serious injury from a shooting, or a physical or psychological threat to the safety or well-being of an individual or community regardless of the type of incident. Moreover, a critical incident can involve any situation or events faced by emergency or public safety personnel, responders, or individual that causes a distressing, dramatic, or profound change or disruption in their physical, physiological, or psychological functioning. There are oftentimes unusually strong emotions attached to the event that have the potential to interfere with that person's ability to function either at the crisis scene or away from it.

Researchers began to find evidence that emergency workers, public safety personnel, responders to crisis situations, rape victims, abused spouses and children, stalking victims, media personnel, as well as individuals who were exposed to a variety of critical incidents (e.g., fire, earthquake, flood, industrial disaster, and workplace violence) also developed short-term crisis reactions.

Short-term crisis reactions include the cataclysms of emotion, in which feelings and thoughts run the gamut and include such diverse symptoms as shock, denial, anger, rage, sadness, confusion, terror, shame, humiliation, grief, sorrow, and even suicidal or homicidal ideation. Other responses include restlessness, fatigue, frustration, fear, guilt, blame, grief, moodiness, sleep disturbance, eating disturbance, muscle tremors or ticks, reactive depression, nightmares, profuse sweating episodes, heart palpitations, vomiting, and diarrhea. Other possible reactions include hypervigilance, paranoia, light and sound aversion, phobic reaction, and problems with concentration or anxiety. Flashbacks and mental images of traumatic events as well as startle responses may also be observed. It is important to consider that these thought processes and reactions are considered to be quite normal and expected with crisis survivors as well as with those assisting them. Some of the described symptoms surface quickly and are readily detectable. However, other symptoms may surface gradually and become what some call long-term crisis reactions. These responses can be masked within other problems such as excessive alcohol, tobacco, and/or drug use. Interpersonal relations can become strained, work-related absenteeism may increase, and, in extreme situations, divorce can be an unfortunate by-product. Survivor guilt is also quite common and can lead to serious depressive illness or neurotic anxiety as well.

After conducting a few more debriefings with the program director, I became certified. My only YouTube contribution is called "Certified 02." I was above average at dealing with suicide, and the director of the program borrowed some of my techniques.

At the next annual regional CISD conference, the director and his second in command cornered me and said, "You know what you have to do, don't you?" I displayed a puzzled look as they continued. "You have to start a CISD team in Eastern Oregon," they said. "We will help you with the training if you come up with a way to pay for it". Less than a year later, I invited the director and his sidekick to spend one expense-paid weekend in Grant County so they could train a dozen or so people on the subject of CISD.

We called the new CISD group the Southeast Oregon Critical Response Team. We affiliated ourselves with the Oregon Critical

Response Team and the Region Six CISD program. As the only certified CISD team leader in the new group, I was responsible for training the other team members. I continued to receive dispatches from the USDA Region Six CISD team, but I was also dispatched by the Oregon Critical Response Team. I used the Oregon Critical Response Team dispatches to train our local team members. I did the Oregon Critical Response Team debriefings on my personal time and never accepted money for the services. It was more important than money.

The first local person I trained was an experienced ambulance chaser and emergency medical technician. Our first dispatch was for a multiple-death auto accident close to the Columbia River. The girl in training was so taken by the course of the debriefing that she cried most of the way home. She was hooked. When I reported the results of the debriefing to the Oregon Critical Response Team, they said no one had ever debriefed forty people at one time before. They further stated that when they interviewed people who had attended the debriefing, all the comments were in the outstanding category. I had set a state record because no one told me to only debrief so many at a time. If they came in the door, I would debrief them. People do lots of things when they don't know they can't.

The CISD trainee position came with some responsibilities, which included acting as a chaser. The chaser would silently observe people in the group for signs of extreme stress and if they spotted someone, they would signal me with a prearranged hand or foot sign. If someone bolted from the CISD circle, the chaser would follow them out the door and say only one thing, one time. Without making physical or eye contact, the chaser would say in a low, steady, and sincere voice, "It's really hard, isn't it"? At that point the chaser would shut up and get a grip on their emotions because the person in stress was about to dump a world of pain in their lap. It worked every time, and in most cases the runner would return to the CISD circle.

I conducted fifty critical incident debriefings while training the local team members. One of the fascinating things I learned had to do with the words "think and feel." If I said, "How do you feel about that?" The people being debriefed would tell me what they thought. If I said, "What do you think about that?" They would tell me how they felt.

I am not a trained mental health professional, and, although I was willing to put myself in harm's way to help others, I lacked the skills to take care of the emotional damage I was inflicting upon myself.

The local CISD team had been trained and I had been conducting debriefings for seven years when I started having vivid, violent dreams as well as withdrawing from my loved ones by building a bunker in the garage. A very clear pattern had been developing concerning the debriefings I rushed to address. A male would be exceeding the speed limit at night while drinking. When he wrecked the car, the unprotected child in the vehicle would die. I was tasked to debrief the emergency responders, and it seemed that every debriefing I went on involved a dead baby. I noticed that I was becoming angry, losing sleep and both waiting for and dreading the next dispatch call. I wrote a poem that disturbed me so much I decided to make an appointment with a local shrink.

Years earlier I had made arrangements with a counselor at the Center for Human Development to help me if I got in a jam. I told him about the debriefings and substance abuse counseling I was doing and asked him if he was willing to give me a hand if I drove off a cliff and had a negative reaction. He instantly agreed to help me any time day or night and gave me all his possible numbers. His name was Buzz.

Buzz had been a lieutenant in Vietnam. He was in charge of a platoon of scout dog tracking teams and he led them with great success. He and I had served in the same National Guard unit many years before. He was a combat veteran and I trusted him. When we met I showed him the following poem and asked what it meant.

I saw a women hit her child in a downtown mall
So I shot her in head with a bowling ball

I think it's going to get better one of these days
I hope I can get better in some small way

I got mad at my boss the other day
So I cut off his arms and threw them away

I hope I'm getting better in some small way
I'm sure I will get better so don't run away

I saw a fat man crowd into line
I said hey sucker your life is mine
I followed him home to meet his wife
And gang raped her at the point of a knife

Buzz chuckled after he read the poem and told me I had grounded myself. He went on to explain that grounding was a process the mind goes through to protect itself after being traumatized anew. Buzz said the debriefings and the constant flow of dead babies and traumatized emergency services personnel was a new source of pain the mind handled by putting the information in the same storage chamber as my traumatizing experiences in Vietnam.

I had awakened the trauma of Vietnam and piled on the trauma of fifty critical incident debriefings. Buzz pointed out that emergency services personnel may respond to one or two death-producing events a year, but I was becoming involved with seven to ten critical incidents a year—and most involved a dead baby. He suggested that I stop doing debriefings in which children were involved. I left our meeting with a clear understanding of the problem and an immediate goal of dropping out of the CISD group. It had been a good run, and the information I gained about trauma and PTSD was essential, but it was time to move on.

The forest service had been good to me up to this point, and I had paid them back by working hard at my timber-marking job and reaching out to bring the drug-free workplace and CISD programs to the forest, community, and Eastern Oregon. Nothing lasts forever, however, and I was about to get into trouble with the forest service, which would help solve another one of my long-term problems.

The job transfer started when a female acquired a position on my district and started sleeping with a long-time seasonal crew member. The job transfer ended when the crew member started showing up for work with instructions for me from the pillow. I got kicked out of the timber department because it was widely determined that I was to blame.

On a designated Monday morning in 1995, I reported to the road department for duty, much to the surprise of the crew boss. Management had failed to inform him that I was coming. Steve, the crew boss, is an outstanding human being. He was deeply religious, but he kept it to himself. He homeschooled his children and taught them how to work and respect others. He showed up for work every day with his boots on and a solid plan of action. He would rather get his hands dirty than spend all day with his head up management's ass. I liked Steve as a person and as a boss.

By the end of the first week on my new job, I hoped that Steve felt like the winner. I showed up ready to work. The PTSD followed or led me, who knows, to the road crew. I would show up early and many times be sitting on the front steps smoking a cigarette when the next person arrived. They would yell out a "howdy" long after I spotted them and way too loud for the early morning. I couldn't make myself cause loud noises in the dark. It violated my PTSD and military training. Noise and light discipline were instilled in my DNA. You whisper in the dark; you don't yell and get stupid. I couldn't say that out loud. I couldn't say anything because it was dark.

Jerry became my mentor on the road crew. He had been a mechanic in the army and had served in Vietnam. Jerry was close to three hundred pounds, but he carried it well. He was confident, steady, and intelligent. He was also a master practical joker with the skills to operate a backhoe, road grader, D8 Cat, dump truck, or eighteen-wheeler semitruck. In my mind Jerry could do anything. We were a good match for a spell: Tom and Jerry.

Jerry was also a lead blaster. That means he was qualified to blow up things. Jerry attended annual training for the blasting recertification and asked if I was interested in attending the class, as he would welcome help on some of his projects. I said yes because this was an opportunity to handle explosives without having people die. My experiences with explosives in Vietnam twenty-five years earlier were mass-casualty events, and I jumped at the chance to change that cycle.

For the next three years I attended the annual explosives training class with Jerry. The second year of training I showed up at the class wearing an American Division baseball cap. The lead instructor was the main explosives expert for the forest service and BLM in all the western United States. He saw my baseball cap and said, "Americal Division, were you in the one ninety-sixth, one ninety-eighth, or the eleventh?" The question took me by surprise because not many people knew the brigades in the Americal division. I would later find out that he was in Vietnam in the same brigade and at the same time I was. He was in a helicopter observing the My Lai massacre while I was on patrol twelve miles west-northwest. He was on the radio talking to Col. Barker when Barker's chopper crashed into a forward air control (FAC) plane killing all nine people aboard both crafts in June 1968, and we were one of the companies dispatched to recover the bodies and equipment. The lead instructor and I had walked the same ground in Vietnam, but we had never met personally before the explosives class.

The plan to learn how to use explosives without people dying worked. No one died. The biggest project I participated in involved using 1,500 pounds of explosives to blow up an abandoned railroad tunnel.

I retired from the forest service as soon as I became eligible under the rules. I do not regret this in the least. I try to keep to myself and learn gardening. Art is an unrewarded passion. I would like to draw, but I am no good at it. I sculpt in plaster and concrete and hike in the wilderness. I do not make noise after dark. My lights are dim.

The Tree Vet

"The painful paradox is that fighting for one's country
can render one unfit to be its citizen."

Dr. Jonathan Shay from the book Achilles in Vietnam

I was a tree vet again this year. Just like the Vietnam veterans in Washington, DC, who hang out in the tree line on the ridge above the bowl that hosts, The Wall. In the early morning hours, they come out of the trees to lay their hands on the names of the dead. They know which panel and line their buddies are on, and they honor their dead with mementos, joints, poems, and unspoken tear-filled words of love and respect.

In past years I occupied a spot in the trees on the southwest corner of the pond at the Parks and Recreation Veterans Memorial in John Day, Oregon. A brown water sailor friend who manned PBRs (Patrol Boat River) in Vietnam joined me sometimes and things were good. I walked from my house and timed it so I arrived at the hide when the crowd was still moving around. Nonmilitary civilians didn't see me because they didn't have their heads on a swivel scanning the tree line both high and low. They are content to look straight ahead or at the person beside them. I moved into position and no one noticed.

Years later a civilian wannabe asked if we minded if he joined us. We minded, but we let him join anyway. The civilian asked stupid questions and made way too much noise as if to yell, "I am in the trees with the vets. I must be cool!" He moved around and gave away our location. He wanted attention, and we were in the trees to avoid the same. The next year the ceremony organizers plugged in a loud speaker so the tree vets could hear. My hide was revealed, so I stopped attending the Veterans Day ceremony for many years.

I visit the Veterans Memorial at the Parks and Recreation's Seventh Street Complex often. I do it in the dark of night or before daylight in the early morning hours. Several years ago I volunteered to spend many days on my knees laying pavers and leveling the sand by dragging a 2X4 over it. We would then compact the sand to make a solid base for the paving stones. I also learned to mix mortar while helping to build a granite podium that would support the engraved marble centerpiece to the monument.

Things came full circle. The memorial started falling apart. In September 2009 the flagpole broke off. In October 2009 I saw activity at the memorial and again volunteered to help with the construction. The same way I volunteered for the draft and Vietnam. The same way I volunteered for ambushes and to walk through the minefield more than once. I volunteered because someone had to.

****

The date is April 19, 1968. I am the fourth person back in the left column. The other column is less than ten yards to my right. We should not be this bunched up. God knows we have hit enough booby traps to learn. I see and hear an explosion to my right front less than fifteen yards away. I drop to the ground, but before my stomach touches I am on my way back up.

This had become familiar. This was the same thing as the explosion of January 13, 1968, when a Bouncing Betty left us with two dead and eight wounded. Zimmerman and I were the next two unwounded in the column and had to walk the line. Today is not much different.

The following is a glossary of terms for the poem "Betty" that was inspired by the January 13, 1968, incident.

Betty: The M16A1 is an antipersonnel mine. When tripped, the mine springs up out of the ground three to five feet before exploding.

Vills: Slang word for villages

R.O.K: Republic of Korea Marines

Point: First man in a column

Ditty bop: Slang word for "passed over" or "walked by"

Sucking hole: Sucking chest wound

Boppin: A dance that came out of the '50s; the Bop

BETTY

Have you heard about Betty
She's a bouncer in the land of Vills
the first time that I met her
was at the base of an old R.O.K. hill

The R.O.K.'s long since departed
some wire and Betty remain
the point ditty bopped right over the top
but not Scully and Hall, what a shame

It's a hot date our first time with Betty
she dropped ten men in a row

the eleventh in line was Zimmerman
learning things he didn't want to know

The Zimmer-man and I
we got to walk the line
I be judging the size of Betty's holes
on the radio with the Captain all the time

We be needing two choppers for this dust off
one bird can't lift all this weight
we have two that are in no hurry
they be lined up at the pearly gate

The Zimmer-man and I
we be boppin down the line
you with the 2" hole in the shoulder
grab your gear and double time

Betty's got one moaning
another is losing his mind
Another with a face full of shrapnel
froze up standing his place in line

The Zimmer-man and I
doing shit we never knew
rifling through packs for poncho's
getting ready for dustoff #2

I don't think I like Betty
she's a fickle bitch at best
she jumps right up all excited

and puts a sucking hole in your chest

She will blow your legs to the left
and the rest of you to the right
she will blow your balls into the next week
and haunt the dreams and your nights

The January 13, 1968, explosion produces ten casualties. To-day's Betty, on April 19, 1968, produces four casualties. We have become experienced grunts at dealing with mass-casualty e vents.

I move to the right column, drop my rucksack, and strap on the PRC-25 radio from my radio telephone operator: "0900, grid square BS533853, Company C request dustoff (medical evacuation helicopter) for two KHA (killed hostile action), two WHA (wounded hostile action) result bouncing Betty."

I walk into the zone making sure the path is clear for the medics. A fucking new guy walking point in the left column has hot steel in his stomach.

The FNG came in on the hash and trash chopper the night before and has been with the company less than fourteen hours. The company put him in first platoon, and first platoon put him on the point in the left column. First day in the bush and the FNG gets hot steel in his stomach, which may result in him going home.

The guy at my feet is dead. The next guy is dead. The next guy, a lieutenant platoon leader, has had his right foot blown off and his right hand does not look good; he will probably lose it. He is moaning from shock and pain. His weapon has been thrown to the right. It is destroyed, useless.

I yell at the FNG to stop running around because he may set off another mine. Sgt. Fox, who will assume command of first platoon because the lieutenant is down, and Zimmerman talk the FNG to safety.

In three days Zimmerman and I will be on our bellies crawling over to Sgt. Fox who will have a bullet in his gut that penetrated through his weapon before entering his body. Battalion said it was automatic-weapons fire, but I was standing four feet away and only remember one round.

Three days after the Sgt. Fox dustoff, Zimmerman, who has gone from PFC to platoon leader in the course of seven days, will be involved in another Bouncing Betty and I will be on the radio calling in a dustoff for him and three others. Charlie Company's first platoon, first squad is getting beat up for the second time in our first four months in country.

A medic asks me to help put one of the dead guys on a poncho so we can drag him to the approaching chopper. I rifle through the guy's rucksack to get a poncho while the medic rolls him onto his back. I find pieces of bone and blood on the inside of the grunt's rucksack. For the first time I look at the dead guy's face. It is my friend John-John.

I am stunned, shocked. This is the day, the hour, and the grid coordinates where the American dream dies for me. Dark clouds invade my mind and a deep numbing pain penetrates my soul. The medic wants me to lift the right side of the body. John-John is pulverized flesh from head to toe, like the gook on the receiving end of a B-52 package. Concussion and shrapnel have transformed his body to the consistency of hammered meat. I can't find anything solid enough to lift.

A year passes, then two, finally I see the middle finger of his right hand. I test it to see if it will stay attached to his body as I lift him. I grab a hand full of bloody pants leg with my right hand and lift the right side of his body off the ground. I pray his body parts do not come off in my hands as I raise my dark broken friend up and onto the poncho.

April 19, 1968: 0900 hours, grid BS533853, I died, the dream ends, no preparation, I be zombie. I died because it was the easiest and fastest way to deal with the problem. I could not move forward while packing the weight of the dead, and I could not leave them behind. I must sacrifice a part of my soul so my body can move on. I don't have time to morn, only to tuck the memory of the mangled bodies into the corners of my mind and keep on humping.

The corners of my mind will meld over time
the visions of the dead come more often
I've recorded their names and absolved them of chains
while I'm busy constructing my own coffin

God laughs at my notions in olive drab, red, and blue. God laughs at me, and you should hope he laughs at you. God decided I wouldn't die. I assure you I went out of my way to prove God wrong.

On July 3, 1968, I returned from my Singapore R & R with a 4X4 orange tarp I planned to use as ground cover in the bush. I sometimes carried this orange tarp on the outside of my rucksack with my Hush puppy shoes flopping against the plastic. I also had a radio antenna sticking above my head while walking point. Laughter is full of colors.

God laughs in colors
I see in black and white
My fears dark and hidden
the laughter filled with light

Forty-one years after God's laughing watercolor wash, I have conducted fifty critical incident debriefings, which provided trauma-related information to more than six hundred people. I have also organized four interventions and talked down two suicides. I have provided substance abuse information to hundreds of people and published the contents of eleven thousand pages of documents for my Old Guard battalion. I hope to someday teach my grandchildren to laugh in colors, and I have helped rebuild the Seventh Street memorial a second time.

On Veterans Day 2010, I found a new hide to be a tree vet. At this year's ceremony no one saw me. I watched the honor guard members fumble with their weapons and get off two of the planned three shots. They never saw the resolute shadow draped around a posted sentry.

Glossary

A&D: Alcohol and drug

ADVA: Americal Division Veterans Association

AK-47: Soviet-pattern 7.62 mm assault rifle

AO: Area of operation

Article 15: The lowest form of punishment imposed by the military.

ARVN: Army of the Republic of Vietnam

B-52: Boeing Stratofortress, jet heavy bomber

Battalion: Four infantry companies plus support, or about one thousand men

Betty: An antipersonnel mine, M16A1. When tripped, the mine springs up out of the ground three to five feet before exploding.

Blood trail: The trail left by someone who has been wounded and then ran away

Body count: The number of claimed enemy killed

Boo coo: Bastardized French from *beaucoup*, meaning "much" or "many"

Brigade: Three to six battalions, or three thousand to six thousand people

Bunkered up: To withdraw into oneself; to become defensive or paranoid

Bush: All the country outside the wire in the Republic of Vietnam

C&C: Command and control helicopter used by the colonel for scouting and observing the companies under his command

Charlie: Vietnamese Communist

Chopper: Helicopter

CISD: Critical incident stress debriefing

Claymore: US directional antipersonnel mine

CO: Commanding officer

Cobra: AH-1 Cobra attack helicopter

Combat assault: Transporting infantry troops to battle in helicopters

Company: Four platoons, with attached FOs, medics, and support. A company may total 182 people.

CP: Command post

C Rations: World War II–era meal, combat, individual ration

Ditty bop: Slang for "passed over" or "walked by"

DMZ: An artificial line established by the United Nations that split Vietnam into two pieces

Duc Pho: Eleventh LIB headquarters in 1968

Dustoff: Medical evacuation helicopter

FAC: Forward air control

Fast mover: Jet

Forward observer: A person who calls for and adjusts artillery or high-angle indirect fire support

Gook: Any Vietnamese

Go to ground: Slang for hiding on the ground after coming under enemy fire; to dig in, to seek cover behind a blade of grass, your buddy, or a chick dressed up like a rice paddy dike on a motorcycle

Grunt: American infantry soldier

Gunship: Heavily armed helicopter

Hash and trash: Resupply chopper sometimes used to conduct a combat assault

Higher-higher: The next person in a rank above you

KHA: Killed hostile action

KIA: Killed in action

Klick: Kilometer

LP: Listening post

Lt.: Lieutenant

LZ: Landing zone

M16: US 5.56 rifle

M60: US 7.62 medium machine gun

M79: 40 mm grenade launcher

MAM: Military-age male

MAF: Military-age female

NCO: Noncommissioned officer

NVA: North Vietnamese army

OP: Observation post

Phoenix project: A CIA-sponsored program that included assassination, kidnapping, torture, murder, and rape under the cover of gathering military intelligence

Point: First man in a column

PTSD: Post-traumatic stress disorder

Puff: A heavily armed C-130 cargo plane used for close air support. This airplane is also called, "Spooky," and sometimes, "Puff".

ROK: Republic of Korea Marines

SEOCOG: Southeast Oregon Council of Governments

SEOCRT: Southeast Oregon Critical Response Team, the team that conducted debriefings for traumatized emergency responders in Southeast Oregon

Shark: Heavily armed attack helicopter

Sucking hole: Sucking chest wound

Vills: Slang for "villages"

Web gear: Web gear has two pieces: the pistol belt that is worn around the waist, and suspenders that attach to the belt in the front and back. The web gear can be used to hang ammo pouches, first aid kits, canteens, and anything else you can think of.

WHA: Wounded hostile action

WIA: Wounded in action

12408445R00118

Made in the USA
Charleston, SC
03 May 2012